U–V

Military Science
Naval Science

Library of Congress Classification
2008

Prepared by the Cataloging Policy and Support Office
Library Services

LIBRARY OF CONGRESS
Cataloging Distribution Service
Washington, D.C.

This edition cumulates all additions and changes to classes U-V through Weekly List 2008/16, dated April 16, 2008. Additions and changes made subsequent to that date are published in weekly lists posted on the World Wide Web at

<http://www.loc.gov/aba/cataloging/classification/weeklylists/>

and are also available in *Classification Web*, the online Web-based edition of the Library of Congress Classification.

Library of Congress Cataloging-in-Publication Data

Library of Congress.
   Library of Congress classification. U-V. Military science. Naval science / prepared by the Cataloging Policy and Support Office Library Services. — 2008 ed.
      p. cm.
   "This edition cumulates all additions and changes to classes U-V through Weekly List 2008/16, dated April 16, 2008. Additions and changes made subsequent to that date are published in weekly lists posted on the World Wide Web ... and are also available in *Classification Web*, the online Web-based edition of the Library of Congress classification."
   Includes index.
   ISBN-13: 978-0-8444-1212-2
   ISBN-10: 0-8444-1212-0
   1. Classification, Library of Congress. 2. Classification—Books—Military art and science. 3. Classification—Books—Naval art and science. 4. Classification—Books—Navigation. I. Library of Congress. Cataloging Policy and Support Office. II. Title. III. Title: Military science. IV. Title: Naval science.
   Z696.U5U 2008   025.4'6355—dc22   2008017489

For sale by the Library of Congress Cataloging Distribution Service,
101 Independence Avenue, S.E., Washington, DC 20541-4912.
Product catalog available on the Web at **www.loc.gov/cds**.

PREFACE

The first edition of Class U, *Military Science*, was published in 1910, the second in 1928, the third in 1952, the fourth in 1974, and the fifth in 1992. The first edition of Class V, *Naval Science*, was published in 1910, the second in 1953, the third in 1974, and the fourth in 1993. A 1996 edition combined classes U and V into a single volume. This 2008 edition of U and V cumulates additions and changes made since the publication of the 1996 edition.

In the Library of Congress Classification schedules, classification numbers or spans of numbers that appear in parentheses are formerly valid numbers that are now obsolete. Numbers or spans that appear in angle brackets are optional numbers that have never been used at the Library of Congress but are provided for other libraries that wish to use them. In most cases, a parenthesized or angle-bracketed number is accompanied by a "see" reference directing the user to the actual number that the Library of Congress currently uses, or a note explaining Library of Congress practice.

Access to the online version of the full Library of Congress Classification is available on the World Wide Web by subscription to *Classification Web*. Details about ordering and pricing may be obtained from the Cataloging Distribution Service at:

<http://www.loc.gov/cds/>

New or revised numbers and captions are added to the L.C. Classification schedules as a result of development proposals made by the cataloging staff of the Library of Congress and cooperating institutions. Upon approval of these proposals by the weekly editorial meeting of the Cataloging Policy and Support Office, new classification records are created or existing records are revised in the master classification database. Weekly lists of newly approved or revised classification numbers and captions are posted on the World Wide Web at:

<http://www.loc.gov/aba/cataloging/classification/weeklylists/>

Milicent Wewerka, senior subject cataloging policy specialist in the Cataloging Policy and Support Office, is responsible for coordinating the overall intellectual and editorial content of classes U an V. Kent Griffiths, assistant editor of classification schedules, is responsible for creating new classification records, maintaining the master database, and creating index terms for the captions.

Thompson A. Yee, Acting Chief
Cataloging Policy and Support Office

April 2008

OUTLINE

TABLES

INDEX

OUTLINE

OUTLINE

OUTLINE

	Military science (General)
	Periodicals and societies. By language of publication
1	English
2	French
3	German
4	Other languages (not A-Z)
7	Congresses
	Almanacs
	By region or country
9	United States
10.A-Z	Other regions or countries, A-Z
11	Army lists. By region or country, A-Z
	For special branches of the service, see UB-UH
	Museums. Exhibitions
13.A1	General works
13.A2-Z	By region or country, A-Z

Under each country:

.x	*General works*
.x2A-.x2Z	*Special. By city, A-Z*

	Collections. Collected works
14	Early through 1700
	1701-
15	Several authors
17	Individual authors
19	Addresses, essays, lectures
20	Facetiae, satire, etc.
	War. Philosophy. Military sociology
	Cf. CB481 War and civilization
	Cf. QA10.8 War and mathematics
	General works
21	Through 1945
21.2	1946-
	Military sociology
21.5	General works
21.7	Mathematical models. Methodology
21.75	Women and the military
	Cf. UB416+ Women in the Armed Forces
22	Ethics. Morale
22.3	Military psychology
	Dictionaries. Encyclopedias
24	General works
25	Dictionaries in two or more languages
26	Military symbols and abbreviations
	History of military science
	For military history, see classes D-F
	Cf. TP268 History of explosives
	Cf. U799+ History of arms and armor

	History of military science -- Continued
27	General works
	Ancient
29	General works
31	Oriental (Egypt, Assyria, etc.)
33	Greek
35	Roman
37	Medieval
	Modern
39	General works
41	19th century
42	20th century
43.A-Z	By region or country, A-Z
	For the history of the military situation, defenses, army, etc., of particular countries see UA21+
45	Historiography
	Biography
	For military personnel identified with military events in the history of a particular country, see classes D-F
	For biography of military engineers see UG127+
51	Collective
	By region or country
	United States
52	Collective
53.A-Z	Individual, A-Z
	Other regions or countries
54.A-Z	Collective. By region or country, A-Z
55.A-Z	Individual, A-Z
	Army clubs. Army and navy clubs
	By region or country
56	United States
57.A-Z	Other American regions or countries, A-Z

Under each country:

.x	*General works*
.x2A-.x2Z	*Special clubs. By name, A-Z*

58	Great Britain
59.A-Z	Other regions or countries, A-Z

Under each country:

.x	*General works*
.x2A-.x2Z	*Special clubs. By place, A-Z*

	General works
101	Early through 1788
	Cf. TP269 Early works on explosives
102	1789-
104	General special
105	Popular works
106	Juvenile works

108	Textbooks. By author
	Including courses of instruction in particular military schools
(109)	Addresses, essays, lectures
	see U19
	Soldiers' handbooks
110	General works
	By region or country
	United States
113	General works
113.5	Confederate States
114.A-.W	States, A-W
115.A-Z	Other regions or countries, A-Z
	Noncommissioned officers' handbooks
120	General works
	By region or country
	United States
123	General works
123.5	Confederate States
124.A-.W	States, A-W
125.A-Z	Other regions or countries, A-Z
	Officers' handbooks
130	General works
	By region or country
	United States
133	General works
133.5	Confederate States
134.A-.W	States, A-W
135.A-Z	Other regions or countries, A-Z
	Handbooks for militia and volunteers
140	General works
	By region or country
	United States
143	General works
143.5	Confederate States
144.A-.W	States, A-W
145.A-Z	Other regions or countries, A-Z
	Military planning
150	General works
	By region or country
	United States
153	General works
153.5	Confederate States
154.A-.W	States, A-W
155.A-Z	Other regions or countries, A-Z
	Strategy
	General works
161	Early through 1788

	Strategy
	General works -- Continued
162	1789-
162.6	Deterrence
163	Miscellaneous topics (not A-Z)
	Tactics
	General works
164	Early through 1810
165	1811-
166	Study and teaching. Training
167	General special
167.5.A-Z	Special topics, A-Z
167.5.A35	Advanced guard
167.5.A37	Airborne operations
167.5.C66	Convoys. Convoy operations
167.5.D37	Deception
167.5.D4	Desert warfare
167.5.E35	Effects-based operations
167.5.E57	Envelopment
167.5.E58	Environmental warfare. War use of weather
167.5.F6	Forest fighting
167.5.H3	Hand-to-hand fighting
	Cf. GV1111+ Human fighting (Sports)
167.5.I85	Island warfare
167.5.J8	Jungle warfare
167.5.L5	Lightning war
167.5.M3	Machine-gun warfare
167.5.M6	Motorized units
167.5.N5	Night fighting
167.5.P6	Polar warfare
167.5.R34	Raids
167.5.S32	Search and rescue operations
167.5.S68	Stability operations
167.5.S7	Street fighting
	War use of weather control see U167.5.E58
167.5.W5	Winter warfare
168	Logistics
169	Drill manuals (all arms)
	Field service
170	General works
	By region or country
	United States
173	General works
173.5	Confederate States
174.A-.W	States, A-W
175.A-Z	Other regions or countries, A-Z
	Encampments

	Encampments -- Continued
180	General works
	By region or country
	United States
183	General works
183.5	Confederate States
184.A-.W	States, A-W
185.A-Z	Other regions or countries, A-Z
	Guard duty, outposts, etc.
190	General works
	By region or country
	United States
193	General works
193.5	Confederate States
194.A-.W	States, A-W
195.A-Z	Other regions or countries, A-Z
200	Debarkation. Landing maneuvers
205	Stream crossing
	Cf. UC320+ Transportation
	Cf. UD317 Infantry
	Cf. UE320 Cavalry
	Cf. UF320 Artillery
	Cf. UG335 Military engineering
210	Skirmishing
215	Rearguard action
220	Reconnaissance. Scouting. Patrols
225	Combat survival. Escape and evasion techniques
230	Riot duty
240	Small wars. Guerrilla warfare. Indian fighting
241	Counterinsurgency. Counter-guerrilla warfare
243	Prolonged war
	Maneuvers (combined arms)
250	General works
	By region or country
	United States
253	General works
253.5	Confederate States
254.A-.W	States, A-W
255.A-Z	Other regions or countries, A-Z
260	Joint operations. Combined operations
261	Amphibious warfare
	Cf. V396+ Military oceanography
262	Commando tactics
263	Atomic warfare

	Atomic weapons
	Class here technical and administrative works
	For works on the nuclear weapons or warfare policy of a single
	nation, see the general military policy of that nation
	Cf. UG1282.A8 Atomic bombs
	Cf. UG1282.N48 Neutron bombs
264	General works
	United States
264.3	General works
264.4.A-Z	By region or state, A-Z
264.5.A-Z	Other regions or countries, A-Z
265	Military expeditions (Overseas, etc.)
270	Peacekeeping forces
	Tactical rides. General staff journeys, etc.
280	General works
	By region or country
	United States
283	General works
283.5	Confederate States
284.A-.W	States, A-W
285.A-Z	Other regions or countries, A-Z
	Maneuver grounds. Camps of instruction. Drill grounds
290	General works
	By region or country
	United States
293	General works
293.5	Confederate States
294.A-.W	States, A-W
294.5.A-Z	Individual United States camps. By name, A-Z
	e.g.
294.5.H8	Humphreys
294.5.P6	Plattsburg
295.A-Z	Other regions or countries, A-Z
	Artillery and rifle ranges
300	General works
	By region or country
	United States
303	General works
303.5	Confederate States
304.A-.W	States, A-W
305.A-Z	Other regions or countries, A-Z
	War games. Kriegsspiel
	Including use of model soldiers
310	General works
310.2	Computer war games

311	Military miniatures and models
	Cf. GV1218.T55 Children's games
	Cf. NK8475.M5 Decorative arts
312	Problems, map maneuvers, etc.
313	Imaginary wars and battles (General)
	For special countries (weakness of national defense, etc.) see UA10+
	Physical training of soldiers
320	General works
	By region or country
	United States
323	General works
323.5	Confederate States
324.A-.W	States, A-W
325.A-Z	Other regions or countries, A-Z
	Military sports
327	General works
328.A-Z	By region or country, A-Z
330	Transmission of orders in the field
	Ceremonies. Honors. Salutes
350	General works
	By region or country
	United States
353	General works
353.5	Confederate States
354.A-.W	States, A-W
355.A-Z	Other regions or countries, A-Z
	Colors. Color guards
360	General works
	By region or country
	United States
363	General works
363.5	Confederate States
364.A-.W	States, A-W
365.A-Z	Other regions or countries, A-Z
	Garrison service
370	General works
	By region or country
	United States
373	General works
373.5	Confederate States
374.A-.W	States, A-W
375.A-Z	Other regions or countries, A-Z
	Safety education and measures in armies
380	General works
	By region or country
	United States

	Safety education and measures in armies
	By region or country
	United States -- Continued
383	General works
383.5	Confederate States
384.A-.W	States, A-W
385.A-Z	Other regions or countries, A-Z
	Military research
390	General works
	By region or country
	United States
393	General works
393.5	General special
	Including human engineering
394.A-Z	Special institutions. By place, A-Z
395.A-Z	Other regions or countries, A-Z
	Military education and training
	History
400	General works
401	Ancient
402	Medieval
403	Modern
	General works
404	Through 1800
	1801-
405	General works
405.5	Juvenile works
	By region or country
	America
407	General works
	United States
408	General works
408.3	General special
	Including training, etc.
408.5	Examinations
	Including training, etc.
409.A-.W	States, A-W
	United States. Military Academy, West Point
(410.A1)	Act of incorporation
	see KF7313-KF7313.55
	Administration
410.C3	Regulations
410.C4	General orders
410.C5	Conduct grades
410.C7	Circulars
410.C8	Memoranda
410.E1	Annual report of Superintendent

	Military education and training
	By region or country
	America
	United States
	United States. Military Academy, West Point
	Administration -- Continued
410.E3	Annual report of Inspectors
410.E4	Annual report of Board of Visitors
410.E45	Special reports, hearings, etc., of Board of Visitors
410.E5	General congressional documents. By date
410.E9	Documents relating to hazing. By date
410.F3	Commencement orations
410.F5	Miscellaneous addresses and speeches
410.F7	Other documents, reports, etc.
	Including semiofficial material
410.F8	Special days and events. By date
410.G3	Information for graduates
410.H2	Rosters of officers, etc. (United States Army)
	Registers
410.H3	Official annual
410.H4	Other official. By date
	Nonofficial
410.H5	Cullum's register
410.H7-.H8	Other
410.J1	Student publications. Annuals, etc.
	Graduate publications
410.K1	Reunions of graduates' associations
410.K3	Bulletins of graduates' associations
410.K5-.K7	Other
410.L1	General works on the academy. Histories
410.L1A1-.L1A5	Official works
410.L3	Illustrated works. Views
	Biography
	Cf. U410.H3+ Registers
410.M1A1-.M1A5	Collective
410.M1A6-.M1Z	Individual, A-Z
410.N1	Class histories. By date
410.P1	Descriptive works. Life at West Point
410.Q1	Miscellaneous topics (not A-Z)
	Including how to get to West Point
	Examination papers
410.R1	General works
410.R3	Entrance examinations
412	National War College, Washington, D.C.
	Located at former site of Army War College
413	Army War College, Carlisle Barracks, Pa.
	Formerly located at Washington, D.C.

Military education and training
By region or country
America
United States -- Continued

415	U.S. Army Command and General Staff College, Fort Leavenworth, Kansas
	Formerly Infantry and Cavalry School, Army Service Schools, etc.
420	Coast Artillery School, Fort Monroe, Va.
425	Engineer School, Fort Belvoir, Va.
428.A-Z	Other government schools. By name, A-Z
	e.g.
428.S8	School of Submarine Defense, Fort Totten, N.Y.
428.5	Reserve Officers' Training Corps (R.O.T.C.)
428.6	Junior R.O.T.C.
428.7	Army Specialized Training Program
	Military instruction in special colleges, etc.
429.A1	General works
429.A2-Z	By name, A-Z
430.A-Z	Private military schools. By name, A-Z
	Under each:

	Official publications
.xA1-.xA4	Serial
.xA5-.xA7	Nonserial
.xA8-.xZ	Other works. By author, A-Z

Military instruction in public schools

435	General works
437.A-.W	States, A-W
438.A-Z	Cities, A-Z
439.A-Z	Military training camps for boys. By name, A-Z
	For works discussing camps of individual states collectively see U409.A+
439.R6	Camp Roosevelt
	Canada
440	General works
442.A-Z	Special subjects, A-Z
443.A-Z	Provinces, A-Z
444.A-Z	Schools. By place, A-Z
	Subarrange each by Table U4
	Mexico
445	General works
447.A-Z	Special subjects, A-Z
448.A-Z	States, A-Z
449.A-Z	Schools. By place, A-Z
	Subarrange each by Table U4
	Central America
450	General works

	Military education and training
	By region or country
	America
	Central America -- Continued
453.A-Z	Countries, A-Z
454.A-Z	Schools. By place, A-Z
	Subarrange each by Table U4
	West Indies
455	General works
457.A-Z	Islands, A-Z
459.A-Z	Schools. By place, A-Z
	Subarrange each by Table U4
	South America
465	General works
	Argentina
466	General works
467	General special
468.A-Z	Schools. By place, A-Z
	Subarrange each by Table U4
	Bolivia
469	General works
470	General special
471.A-Z	Schools. By place, A-Z
	Subarrange each by Table U4
	Brazil
472	General works
473	General special
474.A-Z	Schools. By place, A-Z
	Subarrange each by Table U4
	Chile
475	General works
476	General special
477.A-Z	Schools. By place, A-Z
	Subarrange each by Table U4
	Colombia
478	General works
479	General special
480.A-Z	Schools. By place, A-Z
	Subarrange each by Table U4
	Ecuador
481	General works
482	General special
483.A-Z	Schools. By place, A-Z
	Subarrange each by Table U4
	Guianas
484	Guyana
485	Suriname

	Military education and training
	By region or country
	America
	South America
	Guianas -- Continued
486	French Guiana
487.A-Z	Schools. By place, A-Z
	Subarrange each by Table U4
	Paraguay
488	General works
489	General special
490.A-Z	Schools. By place, A-Z
	Subarrange each by Table U4
	Peru
491	General works
492	General special
493.A-Z	Schools. By place, A-Z
	Subarrange each by Table U4
	Uruguay
494	General works
495	General special
496.A-Z	Schools. By place, A-Z
	Subarrange each by Table U4
	Venezuela
497	General works
498	General special
499.A-Z	Schools. By place, A-Z
	Subarrange each by Table U4
	Europe
505	General works
	Great Britain
510	General works
511	Special periods
512.A-Z	Special subjects, A-Z
512.A5	Artillery
512.C2	Cavalry
512.E3	Economics
512.E5	Military engineering
512.I5	Infantry
512.L2	Language
512.P7	Programmed instruction
512.T5	Technology
513	Examinations (General)
	For examinations of particular schools, see the school
	Royal Military Academy, Woolwich
(518.A1)	Act of incorporation
	see KD6097.W6

Military education and training
By region or country
Europe
Great Britain
Royal Military Academy, Woolwich -- Continued
Administration
Regulations
518.C1   General works

Call number	Description
518.C1	General works
518.C2	Standing orders
518.C3	Respecting admission
518.E1	Annual reports of Superintendent, Commandant, etc.
518.E3	Annual reports of Inspectors or Boards of Visitors
518.E5	Hearings before legislative committees. By date
518.F3	Addresses to students (General)
518.F7	Other documents and reports. By date

Including semiofficial material

Call number	Description
518.G3	Information for graduates

Registers

Call number	Description
518.H1	Official annual
518.H5	Other

Graduate publications

Call number	Description
518.K1	Reunions of graduate associations
518.K3	Class histories, etc.
518.L1	General works. Histories
518.M1A-.M1Z	Biography, A-Z
518.P1	Descriptive works, views, etc.

Examinations and reports

Call number	Description
518.Q1	General works
518.Q3	Entrance
518.Q5	Final

Courses

Call number	Description
518.Q7	General works
518.Q9	Special
518.R1	Miscellaneous topics (not A-Z)

Royal Military College, Sandhurst

Call number	Description
(520.A1)	Act of incorporation

see KD6097.S3

Administration
Regulations

Call number	Description
520.C1	General works
520.C2	Standing orders
520.C3	Respecting admission
520.E1	Annual reports of Superintendent, Commandant, etc.
520.E3	Annual reports of Inspectors or Boards of Visitors
520.E5	Hearings before legislative committees. By date

	Military education and training
	By region or country
	Europe
	Great Britain
	Royal Military College, Sandhurst
	Administration -- Continued
520.F3	Addresses to students (General)
520.F7	Other documents and reports. By date
	Including semiofficial material
520.G3	Information for graduates
	Registers
520.H1	Official annual
520.H5	Other
	Graduate publications
520.K1	Reunions of graduate associations
520.K3	Class histories, etc.
520.L1	General works. Histories
520.M1A-.M1Z	Biography, A-Z
520.P1	Descriptive works, views, etc.
	Examinations and reports
520.Q1	General works
520.Q3	Entrance
520.Q5	Final
	Courses
520.Q7	General works
520.Q9	Special
520.R1	Miscellaneous topics (not A-Z)
	Staff College, Camberley
(525.A1)	Act of incorporation
	see KD6097
	Administration
	Regulations
525.C1	General works
525.C2	Standing orders
525.C3	Respecting admission
525.E1	Annual reports of Superintendent, Commandant, etc.
525.E3	Annual reports of Inspectors or Boards of Visitors
525.E5	Hearings before legislative committees. By date
525.F3	Addresses to students (General)
525.F7	Other documents and reports. By date
	Including semiofficial material
525.G3	Information for graduates
	Registers
525.H1	Official annual
525.H5	Other
	Graduate publications

	Military education and training
	By region or country
	Europe
	Great Britain
	Staff College, Camberley
	Graduate publications -- Continued
525.K1	Reunions of graduate associations
525.K3	Class histories, etc.
525.L1	General works. Histories
525.M1A-.M1Z	Biography, A-Z
525.P1	Descriptive works, views, etc.
	Examinations and reports
525.Q1	General works
525.Q3	Entrance
525.Q5	Final
	Courses
525.Q7	General works
525.Q9	Special
525.R1	Miscellaneous topics (not A-Z)
	School of Musketry, Hythe
(530.A1)	Act of incorporation
	see KD6097
	Administration
	Regulations
530.C1	General works
530.C2	Standing orders
530.C3	Respecting admission
530.E1	Annual reports of Superintendent, Commandant, etc.
530.E3	Annual reports of Inspectors or Boards of Visitors
530.E5	Hearings before legislative committees. By date
530.F3	Addresses to students (General)
530.F7	Other documents and reports. By date
	Including semiofficial material
530.G3	Information for graduates
	Registers
530.H1	Official annual
530.H5	Other
	Graduate publications
530.K1	Reunions of graduate associations
530.K3	Class histories, etc.
530.L1	General works. Histories
530.M1A-.M1Z	Biography, A-Z
530.P1	Descriptive works, views, etc.
	Examinations and reports
530.Q1	General works
530.Q3	Entrance

Military education and training
By region or country
Europe
Great Britain
School of Musketry, Hythe
Examinations and reports -- Continued
530.Q5   Final
Courses
530.Q7   General works
530.Q9   Special
530.R1   Miscellaneous topics (not A-Z)
School of Gunnery, Shoeburyness
(533.A1)   Act of incorporation
see KD6097
Administration
Regulations
533.C1   General works
533.C2   Standing orders
533.C3   Respecting admission
533.E1   Annual reports of Superintendent, Commandant,
etc.
533.E3   Annual reports of Inspectors or Boards of Visitors
533.E5   Hearings before legislative committees. By date
533.F3   Addresses to students (General)
533.F7   Other documents and reports. By date
Including semiofficial material
533.G3   Information for graduates
Registers
533.H1   Official annual
533.H5   Other
Graduate publications
533.K1   Reunions of graduate associations
533.K3   Class histories, etc.
533.L1   General works. Histories
533.M1A-.M1Z   Biography, A-Z
533.P1   Descriptive works, views, etc.
Examinations and reports
533.Q1   General works
533.Q3   Entrance
533.Q5   Final
Courses
533.Q7   General works
533.Q9   Special
533.R1   Miscellaneous topics (not A-Z)
Ordnance College, Woolwich
(535.A1)   Act of incorporation
see KD6097

Military education and training
  By region or country
    Europe
      Great Britain
        Ordnance College, Woolwich -- Continued
          Administration
            Regulations

535.C1	General works
535.C2	Standing orders
535.C3	Respecting admission
535.E1	Annual reports of Superintendent, Commandant, etc.
535.E3	Annual reports of Inspectors or Boards of Visitors
535.E5	Hearings before legislative committees. By date
535.F3	Addresses to students (General)
535.F7	Other documents and reports. By date
	Including semiofficial material
535.G3	Information for graduates

          Registers

535.H1	Official annual
535.H5	Other

          Graduate publications

535.K1	Reunions of graduate associations
535.K3	Class histories, etc.
535.L1	General works. Histories
535.M1A-.M1Z	Biography, A-Z
535.P1	Descriptive works, views, etc.

          Examinations and reports

535.Q1	General works
535.Q3	Entrance
535.Q5	Final

          Courses

535.Q7	General works
535.Q9	Special
535.R1	Miscellaneous topics (not A-Z)

        School of Military Engineering, Chatham

(540.A1)	Act of incorporation
	see KD6097

          Administration
            Regulations

540.C1	General works
540.C2	Standing orders
540.C3	Respecting admission
540.E1	Annual reports of Superintendent, Commandant, etc.
540.E3	Annual reports of Inspectors or Boards of Visitors
540.E5	Hearings before legislative committees. By date

	Military education and training
	By region or country
	Europe
	Great Britain
	School of Military Engineering, Chatham
	Administration -- Continued
540.F3	Addresses to students (General)
540.F7	Other documents and reports. By date
	Including semiofficial material
540.G3	Information for graduates
	Registers
540.H1	Official annual
540.H5	Other
	Graduate publications
540.K1	Reunions of graduate associations
540.K3	Class histories, etc.
540.L1	General works. Histories
540.M1A-.M1Z	Biography, A-Z
540.P1	Descriptive works, views, etc.
	Examinations and reports
540.Q1	General works
540.Q3	Entrance
540.Q5	Final
	Courses
540.Q7	General works
540.Q9	Special
540.R1	Miscellaneous topics (not A-Z)
543.A-Z	Other government military schools. By name, A-Z
	e.g.
543.R6	Royal Garrison Artillery Cadet Schools
545	Aldershot Camp
548.A-Z	Private military schools. By place, A-Z
	e.g.
548.A2	Addiscombe. Royal Indian Military College
549	Military training in universities, public schools, etc.
	Officers' Training Corps
	Boys' units. Apprentices' schools
549.2	General works
549.3.A-Z	Individual units or schools. By place, A-Z
549.5	Ireland. Irish Free State
	Austria. Austria-Hungary
550	General works
551	Special periods
552.A-Z	Special subjects, A-Z
552.5	Examinations
553.A-Z	States, provinces, etc., A-Z

Military education and training
 By region or country
  Europe
   Austria. Austria-Hungary -- Continued
554.A-Z   Schools. By place, A-Z
                   Subarrange each by Table U5
   Belgium
555   General works
556   Special periods
557.A-Z   Special subjects, A-Z
557.5   Examinations
558.A-Z   States, provinces, etc., A-Z
559.A-Z   Schools. By place, A-Z
                   Subarrange each by Table U5
   Denmark
560   General works
561   Special periods
562.A-Z   Special subjects, A-Z
562.5   Examinations
563.A-Z   States, provinces, etc., A-Z
564.A-Z   Schools. By place, A-Z
                   Subarrange each by Table U5
   France
565   General works
566   Special periods
567.A-Z   Special subjects, A-Z
567.5   Examinations
568.A-Z   States, provinces, etc., A-Z
569.A-Z   Schools. By place, A-Z
                   Subarrange each by Table U5
   Germany
      Including West Germany
570   General works
571   Special periods
572.A-Z   Special subjects, A-Z
572.5   Examinations
573.A-Z   States, provinces, etc., A-Z
574.A-Z   Schools. By place, A-Z
                   Subarrange each by Table U5
   East Germany
574.5   General works
574.51   Special periods
574.52.A-Z   Special subjects, A-Z
574.525   Examinations
574.53.A-Z   States, provinces, etc., A-Z
574.54.A-Z   Schools. By place, A-Z
                   Subarrange each by Table U5

Military education and training
By region or country
Europe -- Continued
Greece

575	General works
576	Special periods
577.A-Z	Special subjects, A-Z
577.5	Examinations
578.A-Z	States, provinces, etc., A-Z
579.A-Z	Schools. By place, A-Z
	Subarrange each by Table U5

Netherlands

580	General works
581	Special periods
582.A-Z	Special subjects, A-Z
582.5	Examinations
583.A-Z	States, provinces, etc., A-Z
584.A-Z	Schools. By place, A-Z
	Subarrange each by Table U5

Italy

585	General works
586	Special periods
587.A-Z	Special subjects, A-Z
587.5	Examinations
588.A-Z	States, provinces, etc., A-Z
589.A-Z	Schools. By place, A-Z
	Subarrange each by Table U5

Norway

590	General works
591	Special periods
592.A-Z	Special subjects, A-Z
592.5	Examinations
593.A-Z	States, provinces, etc., A-Z
594.A-Z	Schools. By place, A-Z
	Subarrange each by Table U5

Portugal

595	General works
596	Special periods
597.A-Z	Special subjects, A-Z
597.5	Examinations
598.A-Z	States, provinces, etc., A-Z
599.A-Z	Schools. By place, A-Z
	Subarrange each by Table U5

Soviet Union

600	General works
601	Special periods
602.A-Z	Special subjects, A-Z

	Military education and training
	By region or country
	Europe
	Soviet Union -- Continued
602.5	Examinations
603.A-Z	States, provinces, etc., A-Z
604.A-Z	Schools. By place, A-Z
	Subarrange each by Table U5
	Spain
605	General works
606	Special periods
607.A-Z	Special subjects, A-Z
607.5	Examinations
608.A-Z	States, provinces, etc., A-Z
609.A-Z	Schools. By place, A-Z
	Subarrange each by Table U5
	Sweden
610	General works
611	Special periods
612.A-Z	Special subjects, A-Z
612.5	Examinations
613.A-Z	States, provinces, etc., A-Z
614.A-Z	Schools. By place, A-Z
	Subarrange each by Table U5
	Switzerland
615	General works
616	Special periods
617.A-Z	Special subjects, A-Z
617.5	Examinations
618.A-Z	States, provinces, etc., A-Z
619.A-Z	Schools. By place, A-Z
	Subarrange each by Table U5
	Turkey
620	General works
621	Special periods
622.A-Z	Special subjects, A-Z
622.5	Examinations
623.A-Z	States, provinces, etc., A-Z
624.A-Z	Schools. By place, A-Z
	Subarrange each by Table U5
	Balkan States
625	General works
626	Bulgaria
628	Romania
629	Yugoslavia
630.A-Z	Other countries, A-Z
630.H9	Hungary

	Military education and training
	By region or country -- Continued
	Asia
635	General works
	China
640	General works
641	Special periods
642.A-Z	Special subjects, A-Z
642.5	Examinations
643.A-Z	States, provinces, etc., A-Z
644.A-Z	Schools. By place, A-Z
	Subarrange each by Table U5
	India
645	General works
646	Special periods
647.A-Z	Special subjects, A-Z
647.5	Examinations
648.A-Z	States, provinces, etc., A-Z
649.A-Z	Schools. By place, A-Z
	Subarrange each by Table U5
	Japan
650	General works
651	Special periods
652.A-Z	Special subjects, A-Z
652.5	Examinations
653.A-Z	States, provinces, etc., A-Z
654.A-Z	Schools. By place, A-Z
	Subarrange each by Table U5
	Iran
655	General works
656	Special periods
657.A-Z	Special subjects, A-Z
657.5	Examinations
658.A-Z	States, provinces, etc., A-Z
659.A-Z	Schools. By place, A-Z
	Subarrange each by Table U5
660.A-Z	Other regions or countries, A-Z
	Africa
670	General works
	Egypt
680	General works
681	Special periods
682.A-Z	Special subjects, A-Z
682.5	Examinations
683.A-Z	States, provinces, etc., A-Z
684.A-Z	Schools. By place, A-Z
	Subarrange each by Table U5

	Military education and training
	By region or country
	Africa -- Continued
695.A-Z	Other regions or countries, A-Z
	Australia
700	General works
701	Special periods
702.A-Z	Special subjects, A-Z
702.5	Examinations
703.A-Z	States, provinces, etc., A-Z
704.A-Z	Schools. By place, A-Z
	Subarrange each by Table U5
	New Zealand
705	General works
706	Special periods
707.A-Z	Special subjects, A-Z
707.5	Examinations
708.A-Z	States, provinces, etc., A-Z
709.A-Z	Schools. By place, A-Z
	Subarrange each by Table U5
	Pacific islands
710	General works
711	Special periods
712.A-Z	Special subjects, A-Z
712.5	Examinations
713.A-Z	Islands or groups of islands, etc., A-Z
714.A-Z	Schools. By place, A-Z
	Subarrange each by Table U5
	Nonmilitary education in armies
715	General works
	By region or country
716	United States
717.A-Z	Other regions or countries, A-Z
(719-747)	Military observations on special wars
	see classes D-F
	Military life, manners and customs, antiquities, etc.
	Cf. PN6231.M5 Anecdotes, facetiae, satire, etc.
750	General works
	By period
	Ancient
755	General works
757.A-Z	Special topics, A-Z
	For elephants in ancient warfare see U29+
	Medieval
760	General works
763.A-Z	Special topics, A-Z
	Modern

Military life, manners and customs, antiquities, etc.
    By period
      Modern -- Continued

765	General works
766	American
767	English
768	French
769	German
770	Italian
771	Russian
772	Spanish
773	Other (not A-Z)
790	Military curiosities

        Including collector's manuals

793	Weapons of mass destruction

        Cf. U264+ Nuclear weapons
        Cf. UG447+ Chemical warfare
        Cf. UG447.8 Biological warfare

795	Nonlethal weapons

History of arms and armor
      Cf. GN497.5+ Ethnology
      Cf. NK6600+ Art

799	Periodicals. Societies

    General works

800.A2	Early works through 1800
800.A3-Z	1801-

    Museums. Exhibitions
      For national collections see U818+
      Cf. NK6600+ Art

804.A1	General works
804.A2-Z	By region or country, A-Z

        Under each country:

.x	*General works*
.x2A-.x2Z	*Special. By city, A-Z*

    By period

805	Ancient

      Medieval

810	General works
813.A-Z	Special, A-Z

        e. g.

813.B5	Beowulf
815	Modern

        Cf. UD380+ Infantry
        Cf. UF1+ Artillery

      By region or country

818	United States

        Cf. E98.A65 American Indians

	History of arms and armor
	By region or country -- Continued
819.A-Z	Other American countries, A-Z
	e.g.
819.M6	Mexico
819.5	Eurasia
820.A-Z	Europe, A-Z
	e.g.
820.S7	Spain
821.A-Z	Asia, A-Z
822.A-Z	Africa, A-Z
823	Australia
823.5	New Zealand
	Pacific islands see GN497.5+
825	Armor
	Swords and daggers
850	General works
	History
852	General works
853	Ancient
854	Medieval
855	Modern
856.A-Z	By region or country, A-Z
	Fencing
	Cf. PN2071.F4 Fencing on the stage
860	General works
	Biography
862	Collective
863.A-Z	Individual, A-Z
865	Military sword exercises
	Cf. UD420+ Infantry
	Cf. UE420+ Cavalry
870	Broadsword exercises
871	Battle-axes. Maces
872	Polearms. Lances. Spears
	Arms for throwing projectiles
	By period
	Ancient and medieval
873	General works
875	Catapults, ballistas, etc.
	Bows
	Cf. GN498.B78 Ethnology
	Cf. GV1183+ Archery
877	General works
878	Crossbows
879	Longbows
	Modern

	History of arms and armor
	Arms for throwing projectiles
	By period
	Modern -- Continued
	Guns
	Including history and antiquities only
	For the manufacture of guns (nonmilitary) see TS532+
	For guns (ordnance) see UF530+
880	General works
883	Artillery to 1800/1840
	Cf. UF1+ Artillery
	Small arms
	Cf. UD380+ Infantry
884	General works
	By period
885	Early to 1700/1800
	1700/1800-1860
886	General works
888	Gunflints
889	19th-20th centuries
897.A-Z	By region or country, A-Z
900	Drill manuals for nonmilitary bodies

	Armies: Organization, distribution, military situation
10	General works
10.5	National security
10.7	Civilian-based defense. Social defense. Nonviolent alternative defense
11	Military policy
11.5	Limited war
12	Mutual security programs
12.5	Disarmament inspection. Arms control and nuclear arms control verification
12.8	Guards troops
12.83	Border patrols. Border troops
	Cf. HV7955+ Frontier police
13	General organization of militia
14	Colonial troops. Native troops
	For works on colonial or native troops of specific countries see UA646+
15	Armies of the world. Armies and navies of the world
15.5	Foreign military bases
	For works on foreign military bases of individual countries, see the sending country
	For works on U.S. foreign bases see UA26.A2+
16	Military missions
17	Cost of armaments, budgets, estimates, etc.
	Cf. VA20+ Cost of navies
	Manpower
17.5.A2	General works
17.5.A3-Z	By region or country, A-Z
	Industrial mobilization for war and defense
	For specific wars, see classes D-F
18.A2	General works
18.A3-Z	By region or country, A-Z
19	Military statistics (Theory and method)
	By region or country
21	America
	North America
22	General works
	United States
	General military situation, policy, defenses, etc.
23.A1	Periodicals. Societies
23.A2-Z	General works
23.15	National Security Council
	Department of Defense
23.2	Annual reports, serial documents, etc.
23.3	Special reports, congressional documents, etc.
23.6	History

	By region or country
	North America
	United States -- Continued
23.7	Joint Chiefs of Staff
	United States Army
	Including mechanization of United States Army
24.A1-.A149	Annual reports of War Department
24.A15-.A16	Annual reports of the Department of the Army
24.A17-.A175	Annual reports of the Assistant Secretary of the Army
24.A18-.A19	Annual reports of the Comptroller of the Army
24.A2-.A29	Annual reports of the Adjutant General
24.A3-.A39	Annual reports of the Military Secretary
24.A4-.A49	Annual reports of the Inspector General
24.A5-.A54	Annual reports of the general commanding the army
24.A55-.A675	Annual reports of the Chief of Staff
	Annual reports of the Judge Advocate General see KF7307
24.A7	Miscellaneous documents. By date
25	General works
25.5	Army expenditures and budgets. Accounting
	Distribution, posts, etc.
	Including works on several bases from more than one branch of service
26.A2	General works
26.A3-Z	Special. By place, A-Z
27.A-Z	Divisions, A-Z
	e.g.
27.C2	Department of California
27.P5	Division of the Philippines
	Tactical units
27.3	Armies. By number and author
27.5	Divisions. By number and author
	Infantry
28	General works
29	Regiments. By number and author
	Cavalry. Armor
	Including Armored Force, armored cavalry, mechanized cavalry, air cavalry, airmobile
30	General works
31	Regiments. By number and author
	Artillery
32	General works
33	Batteries, etc. By number and author
34.A-Z	Other special troops. By name, A-Z
	Green Berets see UA34.S64
34.R36	Rangers

	By region or country
	North America
	United States
	United States Army
	Other special troops. By name, A-Z -- Continued
34.S64	Special Forces. Green Berets
	Corps of Engineers, etc. see UG1+
	Medical Corps, etc. see UH20+
	Lists of veterans
37	General works
39.A-.W	By state, A-W
	Not to be confused with state militia
	United States militia, volunteers, and reserves. National Guard
	General works
42.A1-.A59	United States documents
42.A6	Periodicals. Societies
42.A7-Z	Other works. By author
43.A-.W	Adjutant General's reports. By state, A-W
45	Armed Forces women's reserves
	Cf. UA565.W6 United States. Army. Women's Army Corps
	Cf. VA390.A+ United States. Naval Reserve. Women's Reserve
	Cf. VE23.4 United States. Marine Corps Women's Reserve
	By region or state
50-59	Alabama (Table U1)
60-69	Alaska (Table U1)
70-79	Arizona (Table U1)
80-89	Arkansas (Table U1)
90-99	California (Table U1)
100-109	Colorado (Table U1)
110-119	Connecticut (Table U1)
120-129	Delaware (Table U1)
130-139	District of Columbia (Table U1)
140-149	Florida (Table U1)
150-159	Georgia (Table U1)
	Hawaii
	Including history, description, etc.
	For technical works, see UB-UH
159.1	General works. General documents
159.2	Registers. Lists. Rosters
	Infantry
159.3	General works
159.35	Divisions. By number and author

	By region or country
	North America
	United States
	United States militia, volunteers, and reserves. National
	Guard
	By region or state
	Hawaii
	Infantry -- Continued
159.4	Regiments. By number and author
	Cavalry
159.5	General works
159.55	Troops. By number and author
	Artillery
159.6	General works. Field artillery
159.65	Divisions. By letter or number and author
	Coast artillery
159.7	General works
159.75	Divisions. By letter or number and author
	Anti-aircraft artillery
159.77	General works
159.775	Divisions or groups
159.8.A-Z	Organizations. By name, A-Z
159.9	Miscellaneous topics (not A-Z)
160-169	Idaho (Table U1)
170-179	Illinois (Table U1)
	Indian Territory see UA400+
180-189	Indiana (Table U1)
190-199	Iowa (Table U1)
200-209	Kansas (Table U1)
210-219	Kentucky (Table U1)
220-229	Louisiana (Table U1)
230-239	Maine (Table U1)
240-249	Maryland (Table U1)
250-259	Massachusetts (Table U1)
260-269	Michigan (Table U1)
270-279	Minnesota (Table U1)
280-289	Mississippi (Table U1)
290-299	Missouri (Table U1)
300-309	Montana (Table U1)
310-319	Nebraska (Table U1)
320-329	Nevada (Table U1)
	New England
	Including history, description, etc.
	For technical works, see UB-UH
329.1	General works. General documents
329.2	Registers. Lists. Rosters

By region or country
North America
United States
United States militia, volunteers, and reserves. National
Guard
By region or state
New England -- Continued
Infantry
329.3	General works
329.35	Divisions. By number and author
329.4	Regiments. By number and author

Cavalry
329.5	General works
329.55	Troops. By number and author

Artillery
329.6	General works. Field artillery
329.65	Divisions. By letter or number and author

Coast artillery
329.7	General works
329.75	Divisions. By letter or number and author

Anti-aircraft artillery
329.77	General works
329.775	Divisions or groups
329.8.A-Z	Organizations. By name, A-Z
329.9	Miscellaneous topics (not A-Z)
330-339	New Hampshire (Table U1)
340-349	New Jersey (Table U1)
350-359	New Mexico (Table U1)
360-369	New York (Table U1)
370-379	North Carolina (Table U1)
380-389	North Dakota (Table U1)
390-399	Ohio (Table U1)
400-409	Oklahoma (Table U1)
410-419	Oregon (Table U1)
420-429	Pennsylvania (Table U1)
430-439	Rhode Island (Table U1)
440-449	South Carolina (Table U1)
450-459	South Dakota (Table U1)
460-469	Tennessee (Table U1)
470-479	Texas (Table U1)
480-489	Utah (Table U1)
490-499	Vermont (Table U1)
500-509	Virginia (Table U1)
510-519	Washington (Table U1)
520-529	West Virginia (Table U1)
530-539	Wisconsin (Table U1)

	By region or country
	North America
	United States
	United States militia, volunteers, and reserves. National Guard
	By region or state -- Continued
540-549	Wyoming (Table U1)
560.A-Z	Organizations not localized. By name, A-Z
	United States Army auxiliaries, A-Z
	e.g.
565.W6	Women's Army Corps. "WAAC". "WAC"
	Confederate States Army
580	General reports
	e.g.
580.A3	Secretary's reports. By date
583	Special reports
	e. g. Report of Agent of Exchange
585	Collections of general orders
	Canada. British America
600	General works
600.6.A-Z	Distribution posts, etc. By place, A-Z
601.A-Z	Provinces, A-Z
602.A-Z	Organizations. By name, A-Z
602.3	Latin America (General)
	Mexico
603	General works
603.6.A-Z	Distribution, posts, etc. By place, A-Z
604.A-Z	Provinces, A-Z
605.A-Z	Organizations. By name, A-Z
	Central America
606	General works
606.6.A-Z	Distribution, posts, etc. By place, A-Z
607.A-Z	Countries, islands, provinces, etc., A-Z
608.A-Z	Organizations. By name, A-Z
	West Indies
609	General works
609.6.A-Z	Distribution posts, etc. By place, A-Z
610.A-Z	Islands, provinces, etc., A-Z
611.A-Z	Organizations. By name, A-Z
	South America
612	General works
612.5	South Atlantic Ocean
	Argentina
613	General works
613.6.A-Z	Distribution, posts, etc. By place, A-Z
614.A-Z	Provinces, etc., A-Z

	By region or country
	South America
	Argentina -- Continued
615.A-Z	Organizations. By name, A-Z
	Bolivia
616	General works
616.6.A-Z	Distribution, posts, etc. By place, A-Z
617.A-Z	Provinces, etc., A-Z
618.A-Z	Organizations. By name, A-Z
	Brazil
619	General works
619.6.A-Z	Distribution, posts, etc. By place, A-Z
620.A-Z	Provinces, etc., A-Z
621.A-Z	Organizations. By name, A-Z
	Chile
622	General works
622.6.A-Z	Distribution, posts, etc. By place, A-Z
623.A-Z	Provinces, etc., A-Z
624.A-Z	Organizations. By name, A-Z
	Colombia
625	General works
625.6.A-Z	Distribution, posts, etc. By place, A-Z
626.A-Z	Provinces, etc., A-Z
627.A-Z	Organizations. By name, A-Z
	Ecuador
628	General works
628.6.A-Z	Distribution, posts, etc. By place, A-Z
629.A-Z	Provinces, etc., A-Z
630.A-Z	Organizations. By name, A-Z
631	Guyana
632	Suriname
633	French Guiana
	Paraguay
634	General works
634.6.A-Z	Distribution, posts, etc. By place, A-Z
635.A-Z	Provinces, etc., A-Z
636.A-Z	Organizations. By name, A-Z
	Peru
637	General works
637.6.A-Z	Distribution, posts, etc. By place, A-Z
638.A-Z	Provinces, etc., A-Z
639.A-Z	Organizations. By name, A-Z
	Uruguay
640	General works
640.6.A-Z	Distribution, posts, etc. By place, A-Z
641.A-Z	Provinces, etc., A-Z

	By region or country
	South America
	Uruguay -- Continued
642.A-Z	Organizations. By name, A-Z
	Venezuela
643	General works
643.6.A-Z	Distribution, posts, etc. By place, A-Z
644.A-Z	Provinces, etc., A-Z
645.A-Z	Organizations. By name, A-Z
	Europe
646	General works
	North Atlantic Treaty Organization (NATO). Supreme Headquarters, Allied Powers, Europe (SHAPE). European Defense Community
646.3	General works
646.5.A-Z	Participation by individual countries, A-Z
646.53	Baltic Sea Region
646.55	Mediterranean Region
646.6	North Sea Region
646.7	Scandinavia
646.8	Eastern Europe. Warsaw Pact Forces
646.85	North Europe
	Great Britain
647	General military situation, policy, defenses, etc.
648	General documents
	Including reports of War Department and Parliamentary papers
	British Army
649	General organization, history, description, etc.
	Distribution, posts, etc.
	Including works on several bases from more than one branch of service
649.3	General works
649.32.A-Z	Special. By place, A-Z
649.5	Household Division
	Including Household Cavalry and the Brigade of Guards
	Infantry
650	General works
651	Regiments. By number and author
652.A-Z	Regiments. By name, A-Z
	e.g.
652.C6	Coldstream Guards
653	Militia regiments. By number and author
653.5.A-Z	Militia organizations. By name, A-Z
	e.g.
653.5.R8	Royal Sherwood Foresters

	By region or country
	Europe
	Great Britain
	British Army -- Continued
	Cavalry. Armor
654	General works
655	Troops. By number and author
656.A-Z	Troops. By name, A-Z
	e.g.
656.H8	Horse Guards
657	Militia. Yeomanry
657.3	Militia organizations. By number and author
657.5.A-Z	Militia organizations. By name, A-Z
	e.g.
657.5.N7	Norfolk (King's Own Royal Regiment)
	Artillery. Royal Regiment of Artillery
658.A1	General works
658.A5-Z	Divisions, A-Z
	e.g.
658.R5	Royal Field Artillery
658.R6	Royal Garrison Artillery
658.R7	Royal Horse Artillery
658.R8	Royal Malta Artillery
	Militia artillery
658.5.A1	General works
658.5.A2-Z	Special, A-Z
	e.g.
658.5.B5	Bermuda Militia Artillery
658.5.H7	Honorable Artillery Company
659.A-Z	Other special troops. By name, A-Z
	e.g.
	Highland regiments see UA664
659.M2	Maltese Corps
	Royal marines see VE57
	Militia. Yeomanry. Territorial Force. Reserves
661	General works
	Regiments and organizations
	see UA653+
663	Welsh troops and militia
	Including Wales and counties
	For individual regiments, etc., see UA651+
664	Scottish troops and militia
	Including Scotland and counties
	For individual regiments, etc., see UA651+

By region or country
  Europe
    Great Britain
      British Army -- Continued

665	Irish troops and militia
	Including Ireland and counties
	For individual regiments, etc., see UA651+
668	Colonial troops. Native troops
	For individual regiments, etc., see UA840+
	Austria. Austria-Hungary
	Cf. UA829.H9 Hungary
670	General military situation, policy, defenses, etc.
671	General reports
	Army
	Including general organization, history, description, etc.
672	General works
	Infantry
673.A1-.A5	Documents
673.A6-.Z4	General works
673.Z6	Organizations. By number and author
673.Z9A-.Z9Z	Organizations. By name
674	Cavalry. Armor
675	Artillery
676.A-Z	Other special troops, A-Z
677	Militia
678.A-Z	Local, A-Z
679	Colonial troops. Native troops
	Belgium
680	General military situation, policy, defenses, etc.
681	General reports
	Army
	Including general organization, history, description, etc.
682	General works
	Infantry
683.A1-.A5	Documents
683.A6-.Z4	General works
683.Z6	Organizations. By number and author
683.Z9A-.Z9Z	Organizations. By name
684	Cavalry. Armor
685	Artillery
685	Artillery
686.A-Z	Other special troops, A-Z
687	Militia
688.A-Z	Local, A-Z
689	Colonial troops. Native troops
	Denmark

	By region or country
	Europe
	France
	Army
	Infantry -- Continued
703.S97	Swiss regiments
	Tirailleurs indigènes
703.T4	General works
	Tirailleurs algériens
703.T45	General works
703.T5	Regiments. By number and author
	Tirailleurs marocains
703.T65	General works
703.T7	Regiments. By number and author
	Tirailleurs sénégalais
703.T725	General works
703.T73	Regiments. By number and author
	Tirailleurs tunisiens
703.T75	General works
703.T8	Regiments. By number and author
	Zouaves
703.Z5	General works
703.Z6	Regiments. By number and author
703.Z9A-.Z9Z	Other organizations. By name, A-Z
	e.g.
703.Z9R7	Royal danois
	Cavalry. Armor
704.A1-.A5	Documents
704.A6	General works
704.A8	Divisions. By number and author
	Chasseurs à cheval
704.C4	General works
704.C5	Regiments. By number and author
	Chasseurs d'Afrique
704.C6	General works
704.C7	Regiments. By number and author
	Cuirassiers
704.C8	General works
704.C9	Regiments. By number and author
	Dragons
704.D7	General works
704.D8	Regiments. By number and author
	Hussards
704.H8	General works
704.H9	Regiments. By number and author
	Spahis

	By region or country
	Europe
	France
	Army
	Cavalry. Armor
	Spahis -- Continued
704.S7	General works
704.S8	Regiments. By number and author
704.Z9A-.Z9Z	Other organizations. By name, A-Z
	Artillery
705.A1-.A5	Documents
705.A6-.Z4	General works
705.Z5	Bataillons d'artillerie à pied
705.Z6	Regiments. By number and author
706.A-Z	Other special troops, A-Z
706.E52	Engineers
	see UG71
706.G2	Garde impériale (1804-1815)
706.G25	Garde nationale (1789-)
	Garde nationale de Paris see UA708.P3
706.G3	Garde nationale mobile (1848, 1869-1872)
706.G35	Garde nationale mobilisée (1870)
	Garde républicaine see UA708.P3
	Gendarmerie see UB820+
	Infanterie de la marine
706.I6	General works
706.I7	Regiments. By number or name, and author
	Sapeurs-pompiers see TH9551
	Territorial Army
707.A1-.A5	Documents
707.A6-.Z5	General works
707.Z6	Regiments. By number and author
708.A-Z	Local, A-Z
	e.g.
708.P3	Paris. Garde nationale, Garde républicaine, etc.
	Colonies and colonial troops
	For the regiments, etc., of particular colonies, see UA840+
	Cf. UA703.I6+ Infanterie légère d'Afrique
	Cf. UA703.T45+ Tirailleurs algériens, marocains, tunisiens
709.A1-.A5	Documents
709.A6-Z	General works
	Germany
710	General military situation, policy, defenses, etc.
711	General reports

|---|---|
	By region or country
	Europe
	Germany -- Continued
	Army
	Including general organization, history, description, etc.
712	General works
	Infantry
713.A1-.A5	Documents
713.A6-.Z4	General works
713.Z6	Organizations. By number and author
713.Z9A-Z	Organizations. By name
714	Cavalry. Armor
715	Artillery
716.A-Z	Other special troops, A-Z
717	Militia
718.A-Z	Local, A-Z
719	Colonial troops. Native troops
	East Germany
719.3	General military situation, policy, defenses, etc.
	Greece
720	General military situation, policy, defenses, etc.
721	General reports
	Army
	Including general organization, history, description, etc.
722	General works
	Infantry
723.A1-.A5	Documents
723.A6-.Z4	General works
723.Z6	Organizations. By number and author
723.Z9A-Z	Organizations. By name
724	Cavalry. Armor
725	Artillery
726.A-Z	Other special troops, A-Z
727	Militia
728.A-Z	Local, A-Z
729	Colonial troops. Native troops
	Netherlands
730	General military situation, policy, defenses, etc.
731	General reports
	Army
	Including general organization, history, description, etc.
732	General works
	Infantry
733.A1-.A5	Documents
733.A6-.Z4	General works
733.Z6	Organizations. By number and author

By region or country
  Europe
    Netherlands
      Army
        Infantry -- Continued

733.Z9A-Z	Organizations. By name
734	Cavalry. Armor
735	Artillery
736.A-Z	Other special troops, A-Z
737	Militia
738.A-Z	Local, A-Z
739	Colonial troops. Native troops

    Italy

740	General military situation, policy, defenses, etc.
741	General reports

      Army
        Including general organization, history, description, etc.

742	General works

        Infantry

743.A1-.A5	Documents
743.A6-.Z4	General works
743.Z6	Organizations. By number and author
743.Z9A-Z	Organizations. By name
744	Cavalry. Armor
745	Artillery
746.A-Z	Other special troops, A-Z
747	Militia
748.A-Z	Local, A-Z
749	Colonial troops. Native troops

    Vatican City

749.5	Papal guards. Swiss Guard

    Norway

750	General military situation, policy, defenses, etc.
751	General works

      Army
        Including general organization, history, description, etc.

752	General works

        Infantry

753.A1-.A5	Documents
753.A6-.Z4	General works
753.Z6	Organizations. By number and author
753.Z9A-.Z9Z	Organizations. By name
754	Cavalry. Armor
755	Artillery
756.A-Z	Other special troops, A-Z
757	Militia

	By region or country
	Europe
	Norway
	Army -- Continued
758.A-Z	Local, A-Z
759	Colonial troops. Native troops
	Portugal
760	General military situation, policy, defenses, etc.
761	General reports
	Army
	Including general organization, history, description, etc.
762	General works
	Infantry
763.A1-.A5	Documents
763.A6-.Z4	General works
763.Z6	Organizations. By number and author
763.Z9A-.Z9Z	Organizations. By name
764	Cavalry. Armor
765	Artillery
766.A-Z	Other special troops, A-Z
767	Militia
768.A-Z	Local, A-Z
769	Colonial troops. Native troops
	Russia. Soviet Union. Russia (Federation)
	For former Soviet Republics, other than Russia see UA829.A+; UA853.A+
770	General military situation, policy, defenses, etc.
771	General reports
	Army
	Including general organization, history, description, etc.
772	General works
	Infantry
773.A1-.A5	Documents
773.A6-.Z4	General works
773.Z6	Organizations. By number and author
773.Z9A-.Z9Z	Organizations. By name
774	Cavalry. Armor
775	Artillery
776.A-Z	Other special troops, A-Z
776.S64	Special Forces. Voĭska spet͡sial'nogo naznachenii͡a
777	Militia
778.A-Z	Local, A-Z
779	Colonial troops. Native troops
	Spain
780	General military situation, policy, defenses, etc.
781	General reports

By region or country
  Europe
    Spain -- Continued
      Army
        Including general organization, history, description, etc.

782	General works
	Infantry
783.A1-.A5	Documents
783.A6-.Z4	General works
783.Z6	Organizations. By number and author
783.Z9A-Z	Organizations. By name
784	Cavalry. Armor
785	Artillery
786.A-Z	Other special troops, A-Z
787	Militia
788.A-Z	Local, A-Z
789	Colonial troops. Native troops

Sweden

790	General military situation, policy, defenses, etc.
791	General reports

Army
Including general organization, history, description, etc.

792	General works
	Infantry
793.A1-.A5	Documents
793.A6-.Z4	General works
793.Z6	Organizations. By number and author
793.Z9A-Z	Organizations. By name
794	Cavalry. Armor
795	Artillery
796.A-Z	Other special troops, A-Z
797	Militia
798.A-Z	Local, A-Z
799	Colonial troops. Native troops

Switzerland

800	General military situation, policy, defenses, etc.
801	General reports

Army
Including general organization, history, description, etc.

802	General works
	Infantry
803.A1-.A5	Documents
803.A6-.Z4	General works
803.Z6	Organizations. By number and author
803.Z9A-.Z9Z	Organizations. By name
804	Cavalry. Armor

	By region or country
	Asia -- Continued
833.5	Association of Southeast Asian Nations (ASEAN)
	China
835	General military situation, policy, defenses, etc.
836	Reports, etc.
837	Army organization, history, description, etc.
838.A-Z	Arms of the service, A-Z
839.A-Z	States, provinces, etc., A-Z
	India
840	General military situation, policy, defenses, etc.
841	Reports, etc.
842	Army organization, history, description, etc.
843.A-Z	Arms of the service, A-Z
844.A-Z	States, provinces, etc., A-Z
	Japan
845	General military situation, policy, defenses, etc.
846	Reports, etc.
847	Army organization, history, description, etc.
848.A-Z	Arms of the service, A-Z
849.A-Z	States, provinces, etc., A-Z
853.A-Z	Other Asian countries, A-Z
854	Arab countries
854.8	Islamic countries
	Africa
855	General works
855.4	North Africa
855.5	Northeast Africa
855.55	Northwest Africa
855.6	Southern Africa
855.7	Sub-Saharan Africa
	South Africa
856	General military situation, policy, defenses, etc.
856.3	Reports, etc.
856.5	Army organization, history, description, etc.
856.7.A-Z	Arms of the services, A-Z
856.9.A-Z	Provinces, territories, etc., A-Z
	e.g.
856.9.C38	Cape of Good Hope
858	Algeria
859	Cameroon
859.3	Chad
860	Ethiopia
860.5	Kenya
861	Mozambique
861.3	Nigeria

Plans for attack and defense
    By region or country
      United States -- Continued

924.A-.W	By state, A-W
925.A-Z	Other regions or countries, A-Z

Civil defense
    Class here works on all or several aspects of civil defense. For special aspects, see the special topic, e.g. D810.C69, Civil defense in World War II

926.A1	Periodicals. Societies. Congresses
926.A3-Z	General works
926.5	General special

      Including psychological aspects
    By region or country
      United States

927	General works
928.A-Z	By region or state, A-Z
928.5.A-Z	By city, A-Z
929.A-Z	Other regions or countries, A-Z

War damage in industry. Industrial defense
    Class here works on planning to avoid and to minimize war damage to industry. For special aspects, see the special topic

929.5	General works

    By region or country
      United States

929.6	General works
929.7.A-Z	By region or state, A-Z
929.8.A-Z	By city, A-Z
929.9.A-Z	Other regions or countries, A-Z
929.95.A-Z	By industry, A-Z
929.95.A35	Agriculture
929.95.A5	Aluminum industry
929.95.A55	Animal industry
929.95.A87	Atomic power industry
929.95.C5	Chemical industries
929.95.E4	Electric industries
929.95.E43	Electronic data processing departments
929.95.F6	Food industry
929.95.G3	Gas industry
929.95.G7	Grain industry
929.95.I7	Iron and steel industry
929.95.M3	Machinery industry
929.95.M5	Mineral industries
929.95.P4	Petroleum industry
929.95.P93	Public utilities

	War damage in industry. Industrial defense
	By industry, A-Z -- Continued
929.95.R3	Railroads
929.95.T4	Telecommunication
929.95.T5	Textile industry
929.95.T7	Transportation
929.95.W3	Waterworks
930	Strategic lines and bases
	Military communications
	Cf. UB212 Command and control systems
	Cf. UC270+ Transportation
	Cf. UG570+ Military signaling
	Cf. UG590+ Military telegraphy and telephony
	Cf. UH30+ Cyclists
	Cf. UH70 Dispatch carriers
	Cf. UH87+ Use of animals in military service
940	General works
	By region or country
	United States
943	General works
944.A-.W	By state, A-W
945.A-Z	Other regions or countries, A-Z
	Routes of travel. Distances
950	General works
	By region or country
	United States
953	General works
954.A-.W	By state, A-W
955.A-Z	Other regions or countries, A-Z
	Roads. Highways
960	General works
	By region or country
	United States
963	General works
964.A-.W	By state, A-W
965.A-Z	Other regions or countries, A-Z
	Railways see UC310+
	Waterways. Rivers. Canals
970	General works
	By region or country
	United States
973	General works
974.A-.W	By state, A-W
975.A-Z	Other regions or countries, A-Z
979	Other (not A-Z)

980	Telegraphic connections
	Cf. UG590+ Military telegraphy
	Cf. VG70+ Naval telegraphy
	Military geography
	Cf. UG470+ Military topography
985	Periodicals. Societies
990	General works
	By region or country
993	United States
995.A-Z	Other regions or countries, A-Z
	e.g.
995.A6	Alps
	Europe see UA990
997	Preservation of charts, etc.

	Military administration
	Cf. UH740+ Military unions
1	Periodicals. Societies
15	History (General)
	Including history of several countries
21-124	By region or country (Table U2)
	Add country number in Table to UB0
	General works
144	Through 1800
145	1801-1970
146	1971-
147	Military service as a profession
148	Mercenary troops
	Interior administration
	Including post, regiment, company, etc.
150	General works
	By region or country
	United States
153	General works
154.A-.W	By state, A-W
155.A-Z	Other regions or countries, A-Z
	Records, returns, muster rolls, accounts, general correspondence
	Including filing systems
	Cf. UB280+ Correspondence in the field
160	General works
	By region or country
	United States
163	General works
164.A-.W	By state, A-W
165.A-Z	Other regions or countries, A-Z
	Adjutant generals' offices
170	General works
	By region or country
	United States
173	General works
174.A-.W	By state, A-W
175.A-Z	Other regions or countries, A-Z
	Civilian personnel departments
180	General works
	Civil employees
190	General works
	By region or country
	United States
193	General works
194.A-.W	By state, A-W
195.A-Z	Other regions or countries, A-Z

UB

Civilian personnel departments
Civil employees -- Continued
197   Examinations
200   Commanders. Generals. Marshals
210   Command of troops. Leadership
212   Command and control systems
Including C2, C3, and C3I
For Naval command and control systems see VB212
Cf. UA940+ Military communications
Staffs of armies
220   General works
By region or country
United States
223   General works
224.A-.W   By state, A-W
225.A-Z   Other regions or countries, A-Z
Headquarters, aids, adjutants, etc.
230   General works
By region or country
United States
233   General works
234.A-.W   By state, A-W
235.A-Z   Other regions or countries, A-Z
Inspections. Inspectors
240   General works
By region or country
United States
243   General works
244.A-.W   By state, A-W
245.A-Z   Other regions or countries, A-Z
Security measures for defense information
246   General works
By region or country
247   United States
248.A-Z   Other regions or countries, A-Z
Industrial security measures
Cf. HV8290+ Guards. Watchmen
Cf. TH9701+ Burglar proof construction, alarm
equipment, etc.
249.A2   General works
249.A3-Z   By region or country, A-Z
Intelligence
250   General works
251.A-Z   By region or country, A-Z
Electronic data processing of intelligence
255   General works
256.A-Z   By region or country, A-Z

	Intelligence -- Continued
260	Attachés
265	Military interrogation
	Espionage. Spies
270	General works
270.5	Juvenile works
271.A-Z	By region or country, A-Z

Under each country:

.x	*General works*
.x2A-.x2Z	*Individual spies, A-Z*

Cutter by the name of the country responsible for the activity

For spy cases in individual countries, see the country in classes D-F

For spy cases in individual wars, see the war in classes D-F

	Russia. Soviet Union
271.R9	General works
271.R92A-.R92Z	Individual spies, A-Z
	Sabotage
273	General works
274	Equipment

Cf. HV8077+ Identification of weapons

	Psychological warfare. Propaganda

Cf. BF1045.M55 Military aspects of parapsychology

275	General works
	By region or country
276	United States
277.A-Z	Other regions or countries, A-Z
	Preparation of orders. Correspondence in the field. Passes
280	General works
	By region or country
	United States
283	General works
284.A-.W	By state, A-W
285.A-Z	Other regions or countries, A-Z
290	Cryptography. Ciphers
	Enlistment, recruiting, placement, promotion, discharge, etc.
320	General works
321	International relations
	By region or country
	United States
	Documents
323.A2-.A3	Serials. Manuals
323.A31-.A45	Special events
323.A4	Brownsville affray
323.A5	Miscellaneous. By date
323.A6-Z	Nonofficial works
325.A-Z	Other regions or countries, A-Z

	Enlistment, recruiting, placement, promotion, dicharge, etc.
	Medical and physical examination of recruits
330	General works
	By region or country
	United States
333	General works
333.5	Confederate States
334.A-.W	By state, A-W
335.A-Z	Other regions or countries, A-Z
336	Mental examination of recruits
337	Classification of personnel. Military occupational specialists
338	Identification methods
	Compulsory service. Conscription and exemption
	Cf. HD4905.5+ Compulsory nonmilitary service
340	General works
	Conscientious objectors
341	General works
342.A-Z	By region or country, A-Z
	By region or country
	United States
343	General works
343.5	Confederate States
344.A-.W	By state, A-W
345.A-Z	Other regions or countries, A-Z
	Universal service. Universal military training
	Cf. U400+ Military education
350	General works
	By region or country
	United States
353	General works
353.5	Confederate States
354.A-.W	By state, A-W
355.A-Z	Other regions or countries, A-Z
	Provision for veterans
	For general works on veterans of individual wars, see the war in classes D-F
	Cf. UB440+ Retired military personnel
	Employment, education, etc.
356	General works
	By region or country
	United States
357	General works
	Veterans Administration. Dept. of Veterans Affairs
	Official publications
357.52	Serial
357.53	Nonserial
357.56	Other works

	Provision for veterans
	Employment, education, etc.
	By region or country
	United States -- Continued
358.A-.W	By state, A-W
	e.g.
358.H3	Hawaii
359.A-Z	Other countries, islands, etc., A-Z
	e.g.
	Hawaii see UB358.H3
359.P5	Philippines
359.P8	Puerto Rico
	Rehabilitation of the disabled
360	General works
	By region or country
	United States
363	General works
364.A-.W	By state, A-W
364.5.A-Z	By city, A-Z
365.A-Z	Other regions or countries, A-Z
366.A-Z	By occupation, A-Z
	Medical care
368	General works
	By region or country
369	United States
369.5.A-Z	Other regions or countries, A-Z
	Military pensions, bounties, etc. War risk insurance
370	General works
	By region or country
	United States
373	General works
373.5	Confederate States
374.A-.W	By state, A-W
375.A-Z	Other regions or countries, A-Z
	Soldiers' and sailors' homes
	Cf. VB290+ Sailors' homes
380	General works
	By region or country
	United States
382	General works
	National Home
	Discontinued in July, 1930, joined with the Veterans' Bureau and the Bureau of Pensions to form the Veterans' Administration
383.A1-.A49	Documents
383.A5	General works. By author

	Soldiers' and sailors' homes
	By region or country
	United States
	National Home -- Continued
383.A6-Z	Branches, A-Z
	e.g.
383.B3	Bath, Bath, N.Y.
383.C3	Central, Dayton, Ohio
383.E2	Eastern, Togus, Maine
383.S7	Southern, Hampton, Va.
383.2	Army Distaff Hall, Washington (D.C.)
383.5	Confederate soldiers' (and sailors') homes
383.5.A1-.A5	Documents
383.5.A6-Z	General works
	State soldiers' (and sailors') homes
384.A2	General works
384.A3-.W	By state, A-W
	e.g.
384.D5	Washington, D.C. Soldiers Home
385.A-Z	Other regions or countries, A-Z
	Military reservations, cemeteries, etc.
390	General works
	By region or country
	United States
393	General works
393.5	Confederate States
394.A-.W	By state, A-W
395.A-Z	Other regions or countries, A-Z
397	Markers for soldiers' graves
	Provision for soldiers' dependents: families, widows, and orphans
	Cf. UB370+ Pensions, bounties, etc.
	Cf. UB383.2 Army Distaff Hall (Washington, D.C.)
400	General works
	By region or country
	United States
403	General works
403.5	Confederate States
404.A-.W	By state, A-W
405.A-Z	Other regions or countries, A-Z
	Warrant officers. Noncommissioned officers, etc.
407	General works
	By region or country
	United States
408	General works. Armed forces
408.5	Army
409.A-Z	Other regions or countries, a-Z

	Officers
	Including appointments, promotions, retirements, etc.
	For examinations, see U408.5 U513, etc.
410	General works
	By region or country
	United States
	Documents
412.A1-.A2	Serial
412.A4	Special. By date
412.A5-Z	Individual cases, A-Z
	e.g.
412.W8	Wood, Leonard
413	General works
414	Militia and volunteers
414.5	Confederate States
415.A-Z	Other regions or countries, A-Z
	Minorities, women, etc., in armed forces
	Cf. VB320+ Minorities, women, etc., in navies
416	General works
	By region or country
	United States
417	General works
418.A-Z	Individual groups, A-Z
418.A47	African Americans
418.A74	Asian Americans
(418.B69)	Boys
	see UB418.C45
418.C45	Children. Boys
418.G38	Gays
418.H57	Hispanic Americans
	Indians see E98.M5
418.N46	Neopagans
418.T72	Transgender people
418.W65	Women
	Cf. UB383.2 Army Distaff Hall (Washington, D.C.)
419.A-Z	Other regions or countries, A-Z
	Furloughs
420	General works
	By region or country
	United States
423	General works
423.5	Confederate States
424.A-.W	By state, A-W
425.A-Z	Other regions or countries, A-Z
	Rewards, brevets, decorations, medals, etc.
	Cf. UC530+ Badges, insignia, etc. (Clothing and equipment
	of soldiers)

	Rewards, brevets, decorations, medals, etc. -- Continued
430	General works
	By region or country
	United States
	For United States societies of medal winners see E181
433	General works
433.5	Confederate States
434.A-.W	By state, A-W
435.A-Z	Other regions or countries, A-Z
	Retired military personnel
	Including employment, retirement privileges, etc.
	Cf. UB356+ Veterans
440	General works
	By region or country
	United States
	Cf. UB383.2 Army Distaff Hall (Washington, D.C.)
443	General works
444.A-.W	By state, A-W
445.A-Z	Other regions or countries, A-Z
	Medical care
448	General works
	By region or country
449	United States
449.5.A-Z	Other regions or countries, A-Z
(461-736)	Military law (General)
	see class K
(770-775)	Civil law relating to the military
	see class K
(780-789)	Military crimes and offenses
	see class K
(790-795)	Military discipline
	see class K
	Prisons and prisoners
	Including prisoners of war
800	General works
	By region or country
803	United States
	Cf. KF7675 Law of the United States
805.A-Z	Other regions or countries, A-Z
(810-815)	Corporal punishment. Flogging
	see class K
	Military police. Gendarmes
820	General works
825.A-Z	By region or country, A-Z
	Martial law
	see class K

(830-835)	Provost marshals see class K
(840-845)	Judiciary. Administration of military justice see class K
(850-857)	Courts-martial see class K
(860-867)	Courts of inquiry see class K
(870-875)	Military commissions see class K
(880)	Courts of honor. Dueling see class K
(890)	Procedure. Appeals see class K
(900)	Miscellaneous topics (not A-Z) see class K

	Maintenance and transportation
10	General works
12	General special
15	Requisitions (Military)
	Organization of the service
	By region or country
	United States
20	General works
23	By period
	e.g. 1861-1865
	For Confederate States, see UC85+
	Quartermaster's Department
30	Regular reports and other serials
31	Regulations
(31.5)	Laws relating to Quartermaster Corps
	see KF7335.Q2
32	Manuals
33	Special reports
34	Miscellaneous topics (not A-Z)
	Including history, organization, etc.
	Subsistence Department
40	Regular reports
41	Regulations
42	Manuals
43	Special reports
44	Miscellaneous topics (not A-Z)
	Including history, organization, etc.
45	Construction Division
	Military construction operations
46	General works. Armed Forces
	Cf. UC400+ Barracks, quarters, camps
	Cf. UG1+ Military engineering
	Cf. VC420+ Naval barracks, quarters, housing
	Cf. VG590+ Civil engineering (Navy)
47	Real estate service
	Militia quartermasters
50	General works
51.A-.W	By state, A-W
	Militia subsistence departments
61	General works
62.A-.W	By state, A-W
	Paymaster's Department
70	Regular reports of paymaster
71	Regulations
72	Manuals
73	Special reports on the department
	Pay, allowances, etc.

UC

Organization of the service
By region or country
United States
Paymaster's Department
Pay, allowances, etc. -- Continued

74.A1-.A4	Documents
74.A4	Special. By date
74.A5-Z	General works
75	Miscellaneous topics (not A-Z)
	Including history, organization, etc.

Militia pay

80	General works
81.A-.W	By state, A-W

Confederate States

85	Quartermaster's Department. Manuals, regulations, etc.
86	Supplies and transports
87	Pay and allowances
88	Miscellaneous topics (not A-Z)

Other regions or countries
Canada
Cf. UC260+ Supplies and stores

90	Supply and transportation departments
91	Pay and allowances
92	Militia
93.A-Z	By province, etc., A-Z
94-97	Mexico (Table U3)

Central America

98	General works
99.A-Z	By region or country, A-Z

West Indies

104	General works
105.A-Z	By island, A-Z

South America

106	General works
107-110	Argentina (Table U3)
111-114	Bolivia (Table U3)
115-118	Brazil (Table U3)
119-122	Chile (Table U3)
123-126	Colombia (Table U3)
127-130	Ecuador (Table U3)
131	Guyanas
132	Suriname. Dutch Guiana
133	French Guiana
139-142	Paraguay (Table U3)
143-146	Peru (Table U3)
147-150	Uruguay (Table U3)

Organization of the service
 By region or country
  Other regions or countries
   South America -- Continued

151-154	Venezuela (Table U3)
	Europe
158	General works
164-167	Austria (Table U3)
168-171	Belgium (Table U3)
172-175	Denmark (Table U3)
176-179	France (Table U3)
180-183	Germany (Table U3)
	Including West Germany
183.51-.54	East Germany (Table U3)
184-187	Great Britain (Table U3)
188-191	Greece (Table U3)
192-195	Netherlands (Table U3)
196-199	Italy (Table U3)
200-203	Norway (Table U3)
204-207	Portugal (Table U3)
208-211	Russia. Soviet Union (Table U3)
212-215	Spain (Table U3)
216-219	Sweden (Table U3)
220-223	Switzerland (Table U3)
224-227	Turkey (Table U3)
	Balkan States
228	Bulgaria
230	Romania
231	Yugoslavia
233.A-Z	Other European regions or countries, A-Z
	Asia
234	General works
235	China
238	India
241	Japan
245.A-Z	Other Asian regions or countries, A-Z
	Africa
247	General works
250	Egypt
253.A-Z	Other African regions or countries, A-Z
	Australia
255	General works
255.2	Pay and allowances
256.A-Z	By state or territory, A-Z
256.5	New Zealand
	Pacific islands
257	General works

	Transportation
	Pack trains -- Continued
300	General works
	By region or country
	United States
303	General works
	Confederate States see UC86
304.A-Z	By region or state, A-Z
305.A-Z	Other regions or countries, A-Z
	Railroads
310	General works
	By region or country
	United States
313	General works
	Confederate States see UC86
314.A-Z	By region or state, A-Z
315.A-Z	Other regions or countries, A-Z
	Waterways. Troopships. Transports
	Cf. U205 Stream crossing (General)
	Cf. UD317 Stream crossing (Infantry)
	Cf. UE320 Stream crossing (Cavalry and armor)
	Cf. UF320 Stream crossing (Artillery)
	Cf. UG335 Stream crossing (Military engineering)
320	General works
	By region or country
	United States
323	General works
	Confederate States see UC86
324.A-Z	By region or state, A-Z
325.A-Z	Other regions or countries, A-Z
	Air transportation
330	General works
	By region or country
	United States
333	General works
	Confederate States see UC86
334.A-Z	By region or state, A-Z
335.A-Z	Other regions or countries, A-Z
	Mechanical transportation. Motor transportation, traction engines, etc.
	Cf. UF390 Motor transportation of artillery
340	General works
	By region or country
	United States
343	General works
	Confederate States see UC86
344.A-Z	By region or state, A-Z

	Transportation
	Mechanical transportation. Motor transportation, traction engines, etc.
	By region or country -- Continued
345.A-Z	Other regions or countries, A-Z
347	Motorcycles
349	Coolies
350	Camels, elephants, etc.
355	Dogs
	Cf. UH100 Use of dogs in war
360	Skates, snowshoes, etc.
	Barracks. Quarters. Camps
400	General works
	By region or country
	United States
403	General works
	Confederate States see UC86
404.A-Z	By region or state, A-Z
405.A-Z	Other regions or countries, A-Z
410	Billeting
415	House furnishings, etc.
420	Fuel, light, etc.
425	Fires and fire prevention
430	Sewers. Latrines
440	Laundries. Laundering
	Clothing and equipment
460	General works
	By region or country
	United States
463	General works
	Confederate States see UC86
464.A-Z	By region or state, A-Z
465.A-Z	Other regions or countries, A-Z
	Uniforms
480	General works
	By region or country
	United States
483	General works
483.5	Confederate States
484.A-Z	By region or state, A-Z
485.A-Z	Other regions or countries, A-Z
487	Buttons
487.5	Shoulder straps
488	Belts and belt buckles
	Shoes. Leggings. Footwear. Gloves
490	General works
	By region or country

	Clothing and equipment
	Shoes. Leggings. Footwear. Gloves
	By region or country -- Continued
	United States
493	General works
	Confederate States see UC86
494.A-Z	By region or state, A-Z
495.A-Z	Other regions or countries, A-Z
	Headgear
500	General works
	By region or country
	United States
503	General works
	Confederate States see UC86
504.A-Z	By region or state, A-Z
505.A-Z	Other regions or countries, A-Z
510	Tailors. Tailoring
	Equipment
520	General works
	By region or country
	United States
523	General works
	Confederate States see UC86
524.A-Z	By region or state, A-Z
525.A-Z	Other regions or countries, A-Z
529.A-Z	Special, A-Z
529.C2	Canteens
529.C4	Clothing cases
529.H64	Holsters
529.K6	Knapsacks
529.L8	Luggage
	Badges, insignia, etc.
	Cf. UB430+ Decorations, etc.
530	General works
	By region or country
	United States
533	General works
	Confederate States see UC86
534.A-Z	By region or state, A-Z
535.A-Z	Other regions or countries, A-Z
	Equipage. Field kits
540	General works
	By region or country
	United States
543	General works
	Confederate States see UC86
544.A-Z	By region or state, A-Z

	Equipage. Field kits
	By region or country -- Continued
545.A-Z	Other regions or countries, A-Z
	Bedding. Field bunks
550	General works
	By region or country
	United States
553	General works
	Confederate States see UC86
554.A-Z	By region or state, A-Z
555.A-Z	Other regions or countries, A-Z
	Tentage
570	General works
	By region or country
	United States
573	General works
	Confederate States see UC86
574.A-Z	By region or state, A-Z
575.A-Z	Other regions or countries, A-Z
	Tent drills
580	General works
	By region or country
	United States
583	General works
	Confederate States see UC86
584.A-Z	By region or state, A-Z
585.A-Z	Other regions or countries, A-Z
	Standards. Colors. Flags
	Cf. U360+ Colors, color guards (Ceremonies)
590	General works
	By region or country
	United States
593	General works
	Confederate States see UC86
594.A-Z	By region or state, A-Z
595.A-Z	Other regions or countries, A-Z
	Horses. Mules. Remount service
	Cf. UE460+ Cavalry
	Cf. UF370 Artillery
600	General works
	By region or country
	United States
603	General works
603.5	Confederate States
604.A-Z	By region or state, A-Z
605.A-Z	Other regions or countries, A-Z
610	Officers' horses

	Horses. Mules. Remount service -- Continued
620	Horse breeding. Mule breeding
	Farriery
	Including general works on the care of the horse and its equipment
630	General works
	By region or country
	United States
633	General works
633.5	Confederate States
634.A-Z	By region or state, A-Z
635.A-Z	Other regions or countries, A-Z
	Horseshoeing
	Cf. SF907+ Veterinary medicine
640	General works
	By region or country
	United States
643	General works
643.5	Confederate States
644.A-Z	By region or state, A-Z
645.A-Z	Other regions or countries, A-Z
	Blacksmithing, field forges, etc.
650	General works
	By region or country
	United States
653	General works
653.5	Confederate States
654.A-Z	By region or state, A-Z
655.A-Z	Other regions or countries, A-Z
	Forage
660	General works
	By region or country
	United States
663	General works
663.5	Confederate States
664.A-Z	By region or state, A-Z
665.A-Z	Other regions or countries, A-Z
667	Saddlery
670	Stables. Tents for horses
	Transportation of horses
	General, and railway
680	General works
	By region or country
	United States
683	General works
683.5	Confederate States
684.A-Z	By region or state, A-Z

	Horses. Mules. Remount service
	Transportation for horses
	General, and railway
	By region or country
	United States -- Continued
685.A-Z	Other regions or countries, A-Z
	On ships
690	General works
	By region or country
	United States
693	General works
693.5	Confederate States
694.A-Z	By region or state, A-Z
695.A-Z	Other regions or countries, A-Z
	Subsistence
	Cf. HD9000+ Food products (Economic history)
700	General works
	By region or country
	United States
703	General works
703.5	Confederate States
704.A-Z	By region or state, A-Z
705.A-Z	Other regions or countries, A-Z
	Rations
710	General works
	By region or country
	United States
713	General works
713.5	Confederate States
714.A-Z	By region or state, A-Z
715.A-Z	Other regions or countries, A-Z
	Cooking. Messing
	Cf. UH487+ Hospital cooking
720	General works
	By region or country
	United States
723	General works
723.5	Confederate States
724.A-Z	By region or state, A-Z
725.A-Z	Other regions or countries, A-Z
	Bakeries. Field ovens
730	General works
	By region or country
	United States
733	General works
733.5	Confederate States
734.A-Z	By region or state, A-Z

	Subsistence
	Bakeries. Field ovens
	By region or country -- Continued
735.A-Z	Other regions or countries, A-Z
	Officers' clubs and messes
740	General works
	By region or country
	United States
743	General works
743.5	Confederate States
744.A-Z	By region or state, A-Z
745.A-Z	Other regions or countries, A-Z
	Post exchanges. Canteens
750	General works
	By region or country
	United States
753	General works
753.5	Confederate States
754.A-Z	By region or state, A-Z
	Including regimental institutes
755.A-Z	Other regions or countries, A-Z
	Including regimental institutes
760	Refrigerators
770	Slaughterhouses
780	Water supply

Infantry
 Including works on tactics, regulations, etc.
 For histories and reports of special organizations see UA10+
1   Periodicals. Societies
7   Collections. Collected works
10   Organizations (General)
15   History
  Including situation in several countries
21-124   By region or country (Table U2)
  Add country number in table to UD0
 General works
144   Early through 1800
145   1801-
 Manuals
  Cf. U110+ Handbooks for soldiers
150   General works
 By region or country
  United States
153   General works
153.5   Confederate States
154.A-Z   By region or state, A-Z
155.A-Z   Other regions or countries, A-Z
 Tactics. Maneuvers. Drill regulations
  Cf. U169 Drill manuals (all arms)
157   General works
 By region or country
  United States
160   General works
160.5   Confederate States
161   United States militia
161.5   G.A.R. tactics
162.A-Z   By region or state, A-Z
  Canada
163   General works
164   Militia
165.A-Z   By region or province, A-Z
  Mexico
166   General works
167   Militia
168.A-Z   By region or province, A-Z
  Central America
169   General works
170.A-Z   By region or country, A-Z
  West Indies
172   General works
173.A-Z   By island or group of islands, A-Z
  South America

Tactics. Maneuvers. Drill regulations
By region or country
South America -- Continued

175	General works
	Argentina
176	General works
177	Militia
178.A-Z	By region or province, A-Z
	Bolivia
179	General works
180	Militia
181.A-Z	By region or province, A-Z
	Brazil
182	General works
183	Militia
184.A-Z	By region or province, A-Z
	Chile
185	General works
186	Militia
187.A-Z	By region or province, A-Z
	Colombia
188	General works
189	Militia
190.A-Z	By region or province, A-Z
	Ecuador
191	General works
192	Militia
193.A-Z	By region or province, A-Z
195	Guyana
196	Suriname
197	French Guiana
	Paraguay
200	General works
201	Militia
202.A-Z	By region or province, A-Z
	Peru
203	General works
204	Militia
205.A-Z	By region or province, A-Z
	Uruguay
206	General works
207	Militia
208.A-Z	By region or province, A-Z
	Venezuela
209	General works
210	Militia
211.A-Z	By region or province, A-Z

Tactics. Maneuvers. Drill regulations

By region or country -- Continued

Europe

215	General works
	Austria
219	General works
220	Militia
221.A-Z	By region or province, A-Z
	Belgium
222	General works
223	Militia
224.A-Z	By region or province, A-Z
	Denmark
225	General works
226	Militia
227.A-Z	By region or province, A-Z
	France
228	General works
229	Militia
230.A-Z	By region or province, A-Z
	Germany
	Including West Germany
231	General works
232	Militia
233.A-Z	By region or province, A-Z
	East Germany
233.5	General works
233.52	Militia
233.53.A-Z	By region or province, A-Z
	Great Britain
234	General works
235	Militia
236.A-Z	By region or province, A-Z
	Greece
237	General works
238	Militia
239.A-Z	By region or province, A-Z
	Netherlands
240	General works
241	Militia
242.A-Z	By region or province, A-Z
	Italy
243	General works
244	Militia
245.A-Z	By region or province, A-Z
	Norway
246	General works

UD

Tactics. Maneuvers. Drill regulations
By region or country
Europe
Norway -- Continued
247 Militia
248.A-Z By region or province, A-Z
Portugal
249 General works
250 Militia
251.A-Z By region or province, A-Z
Soviet Union
252 General works
253 Militia
254.A-Z By region or province, A-Z
Spain
255 General works
256 Militia
257.A-Z By region or province, A-Z
Sweden
258 General works
259 Militia
260.A-Z By region or province, A-Z
Switzerland
261 General works
262 Militia
263.A-Z By region or province, A-Z
Turkey
264 General works
265 Militia
266.A-Z By region or province, A-Z
269.A-Z Other European countries, A-Z
269.P7 Poland
269.R8 Romania
269.Y8 Yugoslavia
Asia
270 General works
China
271 General works
272 Militia
273.A-Z By region or province, A-Z
India
274 General works
275 Militia
276.A-Z By region or province, A-Z
Japan
277 General works
278 Militia

	Bayonet drill
340	General works
	By region or country
	United States
343	General works
343.5	Confederate States
344.A-Z	By region or state, A-Z
345.A-Z	Other regions or countries, A-Z
	Equipment
370	General works
	By region or country
	United States
373	General works
373.5	Confederate States
374.A-Z	By region or state, A-Z
375.A-Z	Other regions or countries, A-Z
	Small arms
	Cf. TS535+ Gunsmithing
	Cf. UF530+ Ordnance and small arms
380	General works
382	Small arms inspection
	By region or country
	United States
383	General works
383.5	Confederate States
384.A-Z	By region or state, A-Z
385.A-Z	Other regions or countries, A-Z
	Ammunition see UF700
	Rifles. Carbines. Muskets
390	General works
394	Sniper rifles
395.A-Z	Special makes or models, A-Z
395.A16	Ak-47
395.A75	Arisaka Type 99 rifle
395.B23	Bagladeriffel
395.B3	Belgian army carbine (1889 model)
395.E8	Espingole
395.F16	FAL automatic rifle
395.G4	Garand
395.K9	Krag
395.M17	M1 carbine
395.M19	M14
395.M2	M-16
395.M24	M24 sniper weapon system
395.M3	Mauser
395.M67	Mosin-Nagant rifles
395.R45	Remington-Lee

	Small arms
	Rifles. Carbines. Muskets
	Special, A-Z -- Continued
395.R57	Rock Island
395.R6	Ross rifle
395.R9	Rytterkarabin
395.S3	Sharps
395.S37	Simonov carbine
395.S5	Snider
395.S8	Springfield
395.U6	United States magazine rifle
395.W3	Ward-Burton
395.W33	Warner carbines
395.W7	Winchester
396	Shotguns
400	Bayonets
	Pistols. Revolvers
410	General works
	By region or country
	United States
413	General works
413.5	Confederate States
414.A-Z	By region or state, A-Z
415.A-Z	Other regions or countries, A-Z
	Swords, sabers, etc.
420	General works
	By region or country
	United States
423	General works
423.5	Confederate States
424.A-Z	By region or state, A-Z
425.A-Z	Other regions or countries, A-Z
430	Militia. Reserves. Volunteer Rifle Corps
	For history and reports of individual organizations see UA653
	Cf. UA13 General militia organization
	Field service
440	General works
	By region or country
	United States
443	General works
443.5	Confederate States
444.A-Z	By region or state, A-Z
445.A-Z	Other regions or countries, A-Z
	Mounted infantry
450	General works
	By region or country

	Mounted infantry
	By region or country -- Continued
	United States
453	General works
453.5	Confederate States
454.A-Z	By region or state, A-Z
455.A-Z	Other regions or countries, A-Z
	Mountain troops. Mountain warfare
	Cf. UF440+ Mountain artillery
460	General works
	By region or country
	United States
463	General works
463.5	Confederate States
464.A-Z	By region or state, A-Z
465.A-Z	Other regions or countries, A-Z
	Ski troops
470	General works
	By region or country
	United States
473	General works
473.5	Confederate States
474.A-Z	By region or state, A-Z
475.A-Z	Other regions or countries, A-Z
	Airborne troops. Parachute troops
	For transportation by air see UC330+
480	General works
	By region or country
	United States
483	General works
483.5	Confederate States
484.A-Z	By region or state, A-Z
485.A-Z	Other regions or countries, A-Z
	Airmobile operations
490	General works
	By region or country
	United States
493	General works
493.5	Confederate States
494.A-Z	By region or state, A-Z
495.A-Z	Other regions or countries, A-Z

	Cavalry. Armor
	Including horse cavalry, armored cavalry, mechanized cavalry
	Class here works on tactics, regulations, etc.
	For histories and reports of special organizations see UA10+
1	Periodicals. Societies
7	Collections
10	Organization of cavalry (General)
15	History
	Including history of several countries
21-124	By region or country (Table U2)
	Add country number in table to UE0
	Horse cavalry
	General works
144	Early through 1800
145	1801-
147	Armor. Armored cavalry. Mechanized cavalry
	Cf. UG446.5 Tanks, armored cars, etc.
149	Addresses, essays, lectures
	Manuals
150	General works
	By region or country
	United States
153	General works
153.5	Confederate States
154.A-.W	States, A-W
155.A-Z	Other regions or countries, A-Z
	Tactics. Maneuvers. Drill regulations
	Horse cavalry
157	General works
158	Cavalry with artillery
	Cf. UF410 Horse artillery
159	Armor. Armored cavalry. Mechanized cavalry
	By region or country
	United States
160	General works
160.5	Confederate States
161	United States militia
161.5	G.A.R. tactics
162.A-Z	By region or state, A-Z
	Canada
163	General works
164	Militia
165.A-Z	By region or province, A-Z
	Mexico
166	General works
167	Militia
168.A-Z	By region or province, A-Z

Tactics. Maneuvers. Drill regulations
  By region or country -- Continued
    Central America

169	General works
170.A-Z	By region or country, A-Z
	West Indies
172	General works
173.A-Z	By island or group of islands, A-Z
	South America
175	General works
	Argentina
176	General works
177	Militia
178.A-Z	By region or province, A-Z
	Bolivia
179	General works
180	Militia
181.A-Z	By region or province, A-Z
	Brazil
182	General works
183	Militia
184.A-Z	By region or province, A-Z
	Chile
185	General works
186	Militia
187.A-Z	By region or province, A-Z
	Colombia
188	General works
189	Militia
190.A-Z	By region or province, A-Z
	Ecuador
191	General works
192	Militia
193.A-Z	By region or province, A-Z
195	Guyana
196	Suriname
197	French Guiana
	Paraguay
200	General works
201	Militia
202.A-Z	By region or province, A-Z
	Peru
203	General works
204	Militia
205.A-Z	By region or province, A-Z
	Uruguay
206	General works

UE

	Tactics. Maneuvers. Drill regulations
	By region or country
	Asia
	China -- Continued
273.A-Z	By region or province, A-Z
	India
274	General works
275	Militia
276.A-Z	By region or province, A-Z
	Japan
277	General works
278	Militia
279.A-Z	By region or province, A-Z
280.A-Z	Other Asian countries, A-Z
	Africa
285	General works
	Egypt
286	General works
287	Militia
288.A-Z	By region or province, A-Z
292.A-Z	Other African countries, A-Z
	Australia
295	General works
296	Militia
297.A-Z	By region or province, A-Z
298	New Zealand
	Pacific islands
300	General works
302.A-Z	By island or group of islands, A-Z
320	Stream crossing
350	Cavalry outposts
360	Cavalry reconnaissance
	Field service
370	General works
	By region or country
	United States
373	General works
373.5	Confederate States
374.A-.W	States, A-W
375.A-Z	Other regions or countries, A-Z
	Firing instructions
400	General works
	By region or country
	United States
403	General works
403.5	Confederate States
404.A-.W	States, A-W

	Firing instructions
	By region or country
405.A-Z	Other regions or countries, A-Z
	Cavalry sword exercises
	Cf. U860+ Fencing, sword and broadsword exercises
420	General works
	By region or country
	United States
423	General works
423.5	Confederate States
424.A-.W	States, A-W
425.A-Z	Other regions or countries, A-Z
	Training camps
430	General works
	By region or country
	United States
433	General works
433.5	Confederate States
434.A-.W	States, A-W
435.A-Z	Other regions or countries, A-Z
	Equipment. Uniforms
440	General works
	By region or country
	United States
443	General works
443.5	Confederate States
444.A-.W	States, A-W
445.A-Z	Other regions or countries, A-Z
	Horses
	Cf. UC600+ Maintenance and transportation
460	General works
	Equitation. Training
470	General works
	By region or country
	United States
473	General works
473.5	Confederate States
474.A-.W	States, A-W
475.A-.W	Other regions or countries, A-Z
490	Cavalry pioneer service
500	Camelry. Camel troops
	Cf. UF420 Camel batteries

UE

	Artillery
	Class here works on tactics, regulations, etc.
	For histories and reports of special organizations see UA10+
1	Periodicals. Societies
	Museums. Exhibitions
6.A1	General works
6.A2-Z	By region or country, A-Z
7	Collections. Collected works
9	Dictionaries. Encyclopedias
10	Organization (General)
15	History (General)
	Including situation in several countries
21-124	By region or country (Table U2)
	Add country number in table to UF0
(130-135)	Laws relating to ordnance departments
	see class K
	General works
144	Early through 1800
145	1801-
148	Problems, exercises, etc.
	Manuals
150	General works
	By region or country
	United States
153	General works
153.5	Confederate States
154.A-.W	States, A-W
155.A-Z	Other regions or countries, A-Z
	Tactics. Maneuvers. Drill regulations
157	General works
	By region or country
	United States
160	General works
160.5	Confederate States
161	United States militia
161.5	G.A.R. tactics
162.A-Z	By region or state, A-Z
	Canada
163	General works
164	Militia
164.A-Z	By region or province, A-Z
	Mexico
166	General works
167	Militia
168.A-Z	By region or province, A-Z
	Central America
169	General works

Tactics. Maneuvers. Drill regulations
By region or country
Central America -- Continued

170.A-Z	By region or country, A-Z
	West Indies
172	General works
173.A-Z	By island or group of islands, A-Z
	South America
175	General works
	Argentina
176	General works
177	Militia
178.A-Z	By region or province, A-Z
	Bolivia
179	General works
180	Militia
181.A-Z	By region or province, A-Z
	Brazil
182	General works
183	Militia
184.A-Z	By region or province, A-Z
	Chile
185	General works
186	Militia
187.A-Z	By region or province, A-Z
	Colombia
188	General works
189	Militia
190.A-Z	By region or province, A-Z
	Ecuador
191	General works
192	Militia
193.A-Z	By region or province, A-Z
195	Guyana
196	Suriname
197	French Guiana
	Paraguay
200	General works
201	Militia
202.A-Z	By region or province, A-Z
	Peru
203	General works
204	Militia
205.A-Z	By region or province, A-Z
	Uruguay
206	General works
207	Militia

UF

Tactics. Maneuvers. Drill regulations
By region or country
South America
Uruguay -- Continued
208.A-Z   By region or province, A-Z
Venezuela
209   General works
210   Militia
211.A-Z   By region or province, A-Z
Europe
215   General works
Austria
219   General works
220   Militia
221.A-Z   By region or province, A-Z
Belgium
222   General works
223   Militia
224.A-Z   By region or province, A-Z
Denmark
225   General works
226   Militia
227.A-Z   By region or province, A-Z
France
228   General works
229   Militia
230.A-Z   By region or province, A-Z
Germany
Including West Germany
231   General works
232   Militia
233.A-Z   By region or province, A-Z
East Germany
233.5   General works
233.52   Militia
233.53.A-Z   By region or province, A-Z
Great Britain
234   General works
235   Militia
236.A-Z   By region or province, A-Z
Greece
237   General works
238   Militia
239.A-Z   By region or province, A-Z
Netherlands
240   General works
241   Militia

	Tactics. Maneuvers. Drill regulations
	By region or country
	Europe
	Greece
242.A-Z	By region or province, A-Z
	Italy
243	General works
244	Militia
245.A-Z	By region or province, A-Z
	Norway
246	General works
247	Militia
248.A-Z	By region or province, A-Z
	Portugal
249	General works
250	Militia
251.A-Z	By region or province, A-Z
	Soviet Union
252	General works
253	Militia
254.A-Z	By region or province, A-Z
	Spain
255	General works
256	Militia
257.A-Z	By region or province, A-Z
	Sweden
258	General works
259	Militia
260.A-Z	By region or province, A-Z
	Switzerland
261	General works
262	Militia
263.A-Z	By region or province, A-Z
	Turkey
264	General works
265	Militia
266.A-Z	By region or province, A-Z
269.A-Z	Other European countries, A-Z
	e.g.
269.P7	Poland
269.R8	Romania
269.Y8	Yugoslavia
	Asia
270	General works
	China
271	General works
272	Militia

	Tactics. Maneuvers. Drill regulations
	By region or country
	Asia
	China -- Continued
273.A-Z	By region or province, A-Z
	India
274	General works
275	Militia
276.A-Z	By region or province, A-Z
	Japan
277	General works
278	Militia
279.A-Z	By region or province, A-Z
280.A-Z	Other Asian countries, A-Z
	Africa
285	General works
	Egypt
286	General works
287	Militia
288.A-Z	By region or province, A-Z
292.A-Z	Other African countries, A-Z
	Australia
295	General works
296	Militia
297.A-Z	By region or province, A-Z
298	New Zealand
	Pacific islands
300	General works
302.A-Z	By island or group of islands, A-Z
320	Stream crossing
	Target practice
340	General works
	By region or country
	United States
343	General works
343.5	Confederate States
344.A-.W	States, A-W
345.A-Z	Other regions or countries, A-Z
	Field service
350	General works
	By region or country
	United States
353	General works
353.5	Confederate States
354.A-.W	States, A-W
355.A-Z	Other regions or countries, A-Z

356	Artillery reserves and militia
	For history and reports of individual organizations, see UA56
	UA657+ etc.
	Equipment, harness, etc
360	General works
	By region or country
	United States
363	General works
363.5	Confederate States
364.A-.W	States, A-W
365.A-Z	Other regions or countries, A-Z
370	Horses
	Cf. UC600+ Maintenance and transportation
	Wagons, carts, etc.
	Cf. UF640+ Gun carriages, etc.
380	General works
	By region or country
	United States
383	General works
383.5	Confederate States
384.A-.W	States, A-W
385.A-Z	Other regions or countries, A-Z
390	Motor transportation
	Field artillery
	For target practice see UF340+
400	General works
	By region or country
	United States
403	General works
403.5	Confederate States
404.A-.W	States, A-W
405.A-Z	Other regions or countries, A-Z
410	Horse artillery
	Cf. UE158 Cavalry with artillery
420	Camel batteries
430	Elephant batteries
	Mountain artillery
	Including use of artillery in mountains
440	General works
	By region or country
	United States
443	General works
443.5	Confederate States
444.A-.W	States, A-W
445.A-Z	Other regions or countries, A-Z
	Seacoast artillery
450	General works

	Seacoast artillery -- Continued
	By region or country
	United States
	Cf. U428.S8 School of Submarine Defense, Fort Totten, N.Y.
453	General works
453.5	Confederate States
454.A-.W	States, A-W
455.A-Z	Other regions or countries, A-Z
	Siege artillery
460	General works
	By region or country
	United States
463	General works
463.5	Confederate States
464.A-.W	States, A-W
465.A-Z	Other regions or countries, A-Z
	Howitzer artillery. Mortar batteries
470	General works
	By region or country
	United States
473	General works
473.5	Confederate States
474.A-.W	States, A-W
475.A-Z	Other regions or countries, A-Z
	Garrison artillery. Fortress artillery
480	General works
	By region or country
	United States
483	General works
483.5	Confederate States
484.A-.W	States, A-W
485.A-Z	Other regions or countries, A-Z
	Railway artillery
490	General works
	By region or country
	United States
493	General works
493.5	Confederate States
494.A-.W	States, A-W
495.A-Z	Other regions or countries, A-Z
	Weapons systems
500	General works
	By region or country
	United States
503	General works
503.5	Confederate States

	Weapons systems
	By region or country
	United States -- Continued
504.A-.W	States, A-W
505.A-Z	Other regions or countries, A-Z
	Precision guided munitions
510	General works
	By region or country
	United States
513	General works
514.A-.W	States, A-W
515.A-Z	Other regions or countries, A-Z
	Ordnance and small arms
	Cf. UD380+ Infantry small arms
520	General works
	By region or country
	United States
523	General works
523.5	Confederate States
524.A-.W	States, A-W
525.A-Z	Other regions or countries, A-Z
	Research
526	General works
	By region or country
526.3	United States
526.5.A-Z	Other regions or countries, A-Z
527	Study and teaching
	Manufacture
	Including reports of ordnance factories
530	General works
	By region or country
	United States
533	General works
533.5	Confederate States
534.A-.W	States, A-W
535.A-Z	Other regions or countries, A-Z
537.A-Z	By manufacturer, A-Z
	Arsenals, magazines, armories, etc.
540	General works
	By region or country
	United States
543.A3	General works
543.A4-Z	Individual arsenals. By place, A-Z
543.5	Confederate States
544.A-.W	States, A-W
545.A-Z	Other regions or countries, A-Z
	Ordnance stores, accounts, etc.

	Ordnance stores, accounts, etc. -- Continued
550	General works
	By region or country
	United States
553	General works
553.5	Confederate States
554.A-.W	States, A-W
555.A-Z	Other regions or countries, A-Z
	Ordnance material (Ordnance proper)
560	General works
561	General special
	Including matériel for accompaniment of infantry
	By region or country
	United States
	Gun handbooks
563.A4	By mm. or cm.
	Subarranged by date, e.g. UF563.A4 75 mm 1920
563.A5	By inches
	Subarranged by date, e.g. UF563.A5 4.5 in 1943
563.A6	By pounds
	Subarranged by date, e.g. UF563.A6 15 pr 1907
563.A7-.A8	By class
	Subarranged by date
	For guns of a specific caliber or weight, see UF563.A4, UF563.A5, UF563.A6
563.A7	Coast guns
563.A75	Mortars
563.A76	Railway gun matériel
563.A77	Trench warfare matériel
563.A8	Subcaliber guns
563.A9-Z	General works
565.A-Z	Other regions or countries, A-Z
	e.g.
	Great Britain gun handbooks
565.G7	By inches
	Arrange different editions by date
	Further subdivision is made by adding the following letters as needed: B.L. Breech loading; M.L. Muzzle loading; Q.F. Quick firing; H. Hotchkiss; N. Nordenfelt
	Guns of different marks have the numbers added in parentheses; thus for marks II to IV, add (2)-(4)

Ordnance material (Ordnance proper)
  By region or country
    Other regions or countries, A-Z
      Great Britain gun handbooks -- Continued

565.G72	By pounds
	Arrange different editions by date
	Further subdivision is made by adding the following letters as needed: B.L. Breech loading; M.L. Muzzle loading; Q.F. Quick firing; H. Hotchkiss; N. Nordenfelt
	Guns of different marks have the numbers added in parentheses; thus for marks II to IV add (2)-(4)
	Machine guns
620.A2	General works
620.A3-Z	Special types, A-Z
620.B6	Browning
620.C6	Colt
620.D4	Degtiarev
620.G2	Gardner and Nordenfelt
620.G6	Goriūnov
620.H8	Hotchkiss
620.L5	Lewis
620.M4	Maxim
620.M6	MG-34
620.M7	Mitrailleuse
620.N8	Nordenfelt
620.O92	Owen
620.R45	Reising
620.S8	Sten machine carbines
620.T5	Thompson
620.U6	United States automatic .30-inch (1904 and 1909 models)
620.U9	Uzi
620.V4	Vickers
625	Antiaircraft guns
	Cf. UG730+ Air defenses
628	Antitank weapons
630	Other types of guns (not A-Z)
	Gun carriages, caissons, limbers, etc.
	Cf. UF380+ Wagons, carts, etc.
640	General works
	By region or country
	United States
643	General works
643.5	Confederate States
644.A-.W	States, A-W
645.A-Z	Other regions or countries, A-Z

	Ordnance material (Ordnance proper)
	Gun carriages, caissons, limbers, etc. -- Continued
650	Disappearing gun carriages
652	Self-propelled gun carriages. Tracklaying tractors, etc.
655	Railway gun cars
	For gun cars of the United States see UF563.A76
	For gun cars of special countries see UF565.A+
656	Recoilless rifles
660	Revolving cupolas, portable gun shelters, etc.
	Firing instructions
670	General works
	By region or country
	United States
673	General works
673.5	Confederate States
674.A-.W	States, A-W
675.A-Z	Other regions or countries, A-Z
700	Ammunition
	Cartridges
740	General works
	By region or country
	United States
743	General works
743.5	Confederate States
744.A-.W	States, A-W
745.A-Z	Other regions or countries, A-Z
	Projectiles
750	General works
	By region or country
	United States
753	General works
753.5	Confederate States
754.A-.W	States, A-W
755.A-Z	Other regions or countries, A-Z
760	Shrapnel, shells, etc.
765	Grenades. Grenade launchers
767	Projectiles for aircraft. Bombs, etc.
770	Bullets
780	Firing devices: Percussion caps, primers, etc.
	Gunnery
800	General works
805	Aerial observations and artillery
810	Results of firing tests. Deviations, etc.
	Ballistics. Velocities and motions of projectiles
820	General works
823	Interior ballistics
825	Exterior ballistics

	Ballistics. Velocities and motions of projectiles -- Continued
830.A-Z	Ballistic instruments, A-Z
830.C4	Chronograph and chronoscope
830.C5	Clepsydra
830.G9	Gyroscopic instruments
840	Ballistic photography. Photochronograph
845	Telescopes and binoculars (Military)
	Artillery instruments. Fire control, etc.
848	General works
849	Optics. Optical instruments and equipment
	Range finders
850.A2	General works
850.A3-Z	Special. By name, A-Z
850.A9	Azimuth instrument
850.D4	Depression range finder
850.L4	Le Boulengé télémètre
850.M2	Marindin range finder
850.M5	Mekometer
850.N8	Nolan range finder
850.R6	Rochon micrometer telescope
850.R7	Roksandié range finder
850.S6	Sound ranging instruments
850.T4	Telemeter
850.W3	Watkin range finder
850.W5	Weldon range finder
853	Position finders
854	Sights for firearms
855	Telescopic sights
856.A-Z	Other artillery instruments, A-Z
857	Range tables
	Military explosives and pyrotechnics
	Cf. TP270+ Explosives (General)
860	General works
870	Explosions, force of powders, etc.
	Including measurement of powder pressure in cannon
880	Rockets
	Cf. UG1310+ Guided missiles (Air Force)
890	Ordnance tests
	Cf. UG408+ Testing of iron and steel for land defenses
	Cf. V910+ Armor plate tests
	Cf. VF540 Naval ordnance tests
900	Resistance to projectiles
910	Bulletproof clothing and materials

Military engineering
1 Periodicals. Societies
5 Congresses
Museums. Exhibitions
6.A1 General works
6.A2-Z By region or country, A-Z
Under each country:
.x *General works*
.x2A-.x2Z *Special. By city, A-Z*
7 Collections. Collected works
15 History
Including history of several countries
21-124 By region or country
21 America
North America
22 General works
United States
23 General works
23.5 Confederate States
24.A-.W By state, A-W
25 Regiments of United States Army. By number
Canada
26.A-.Z5 General works
26.Z6 Individual regiments. By number
27.A-Z By state, province, etc., A-Z
27.5 Latin America (General)
Mexico
28.A-.Z5 General works
28.Z6 Individual regiments. By number
29.A-Z By state, province, etc., A-Z
Central America
30 General works
31.A-Z By country, A-Z
West Indies
32 General works
33.A-Z By country or island, A-Z
South America
34 General works
Argentina
36.A-.Z5 General works
36.Z6 Individual regiments. By number
37.A-Z By state, province, etc., A-Z
Bolivia
38.A-.Z5 General works
38.Z6 Individual regiments. By number
39.A-Z By state, province, etc., A-Z
Brazil

	By region or country
	South America
	Brazil -- Continued
41.A-.Z5	General works
41.Z6	Individual regiments. By number
42.A-Z	By state, province, etc., A-Z
	Chile
43.A-.Z5	General works
43.Z6	Individual regiments. By number
44.A-Z	By state, province, etc., A-Z
	Colombia
45.A-.Z5	General works
45.Z6	Individual regiments. By number
46.A-Z	By state, province, etc., A-Z
	Ecuador
47.A-.Z5	General works
47.Z6	Individual regiments. By number
48.A-Z	By state, province, etc., A-Z
	Guianas
49	General works
49.5	Suriname. Dutch Guiana
50	French Guiana
51	Paraguay
52	Peru
53	Uruguay
54	Venezuela
	Europe
55	General works
	Great Britain
57	General works
58	Special periods. By date
59	England and Wales
61	Scotland
63	Northern Ireland
64.A-Z	Cities (or other special), A-Z
	Austria
65.A-.Z5	General works
65.Z6	Individual regiments. By number
66.A-Z	By state, province, etc., A-Z
	Belgium
67.A-.Z5	General works
67.Z6	Individual regiments. By number
68.A-Z	By state, province, etc., A-Z
	Denmark
69.A-.Z5	General works
69.Z6	Individual regiments. By number
70.A-Z	By state, province, etc., A-Z

	By region or country
	Europe -- Continued
	France
71.A-.Z5	General works
71.Z6	Individual regiments. By number
72.A-Z	By state, province, etc., A-Z
	Germany
	Including West Germany
73.A-.Z5	General works
73.Z6	Individual regiments. By number
74.A-Z	By state, province, etc., A-Z
74.5	East Germany
	Greece
75.A-.Z5	General works
75.Z6	Individual regiments. By number
76.A-Z	By state, province, etc., A-Z
76.5	Ireland (Eire)
	Netherlands
77.A-.Z5	General works
77.Z6	Individual regiments. By number
78.A-Z	By state, province, etc., A-Z
	Italy
79.A-.Z5	General works
79.Z6	Individual regiments. By number
80.A-Z	By state, province, etc., A-Z
	Norway
81.A-.Z5	General works
81.Z6	Individual regiments. By number
82.A-Z	By state, province, etc., A-Z
	Portugal
83.A-.Z5	General works
83.Z6	Individual regiments. By number
84.A-Z	By state, province, etc., A-Z
	Soviet Union
85.A-.Z5	General works
85.Z6	Individual regiments. By number
86.A-Z	By state, province, etc., A-Z
86.5	Scandinavia (General)
	Spain
87.A-.Z5	General works
87.Z6	Individual regiments. By number
88.A-Z	By state, province, etc., A-Z
	Sweden
89.A-.Z5	General works
89.Z6	Individual regiments. By number
90.A-Z	By state, province, etc., A-Z
	Switzerland

	By region or country
	Europe
	Switzerland -- Continued
91.A-.Z5	General works
91.Z6	Individual regiments. By number
92.A-Z	By state, province, etc., A-Z
	Turkey see UG111+
95.A-Z	Other European countries, A-Z
	Asia
99	General works
	China
101.A-.Z5	General works
101.Z6	Individual regiments. By number
102.A-Z	By state, province, etc., A-Z
	India
103.A-.Z5	General works
103.Z6	Individual regiments. By number
104.A-Z	By state, province, etc., A-Z
	Japan
105.A-.Z5	General works
105.Z6	Individual regiments. By number
106.A-Z	By state, province, etc., A-Z
	Iran
107.A-.Z5	General works
107.Z6	Individual regiments. By number
108.A-Z	By state, province, etc., A-Z
	Soviet Union in Asia. Siberia
109.A-.Z5	General works
109.Z6	Individual regiments. By number
110.A-Z	By state, province, etc., A-Z
	Turkey
111.A-.Z5	General works
111.Z6	Individual regiments. By number
112.A-Z	By state, province, etc., A-Z
113.A-Z	Other Asian countries, A-Z
	Africa
115	General works
	Egypt
117.A-.Z5	General works
117.Z6	Individual regiments. By number
118.A-Z	By state, province, etc., A-Z
119.A-116.Z	Other African countries, A-Z
	Australia
121.A-.Z5	General works
121.Z6	Individual regiments. By number
122.A-Z	By state, province, etc., A-Z
122.5	New Zealand

	By region or country -- Continued
	Pacific islands
123	General works
124.A-Z	By island or group of islands, A-Z
	Biography
127	Collective
	For biography by region or country see UG21+
128.A-Z	Individual, A-Z
(130-135)	Laws relating to engineer corps
	see class K
	General works
144	Early through 1800
145	1801-
147	General special
	Manuals
150	General works
	By region or country
153	United States
155.A-Z	Other regions or countries, A-Z
156	Addresses, essays, lectures
157	Study and teaching
	Tactics and regulations
	By region or country
	United States
160	General works
160.5	Confederate States
161	United States militia
161.5	G.A.R. tactics
162.A-Z	By region or state, A-Z
	Canada
163	General works
164	Militia
165.A-Z	By region or province, A-Z
	Mexico
166	General works
167	Milita
168.A-Z	By region or province, A-Z
	Central America
169	General works
170.A-Z	By region or country, A-Z
	West Indies
172	General works
173.A-Z	By island or group of islands, A-Z
	South America
175	General works
	Argentina
176	General works

Tactics and regulations
   By region or country
      South America
         Argentina -- Continued

177	Militia
178.A-Z	By region or province, A-Z
	Bolivia
179	General works
180	Militia
181.A-Z	By region or province, A-Z
	Brazil
182	General works
183	Militia
184.A-Z	By region or province, A-Z
	Chile
185	General works
186	Militia
187.A-Z	By region or province, A-Z
	Colombia
188	General works
189	Militia
190.A-Z	By region or province, A-Z
	Ecuador
191	General works
192	Militia
193.A-Z	By region or province, A-Z
195	Guyana
196	Suriname
197	French Guiana
	Paraguay
200	General works
201	Militia
202.A-Z	By region or province, A-Z
	Peru
203	General works
204	Militia
205.A-Z	By region or province, A-Z
	Uruguay
206	General works
207	Militia
208.A-Z	By region or province, A-Z
	Venezuela
209	General works
210	Militia
211.A-Z	By region or province, A-Z
	Europe
215	General works

Tactics and regulations
By region or country
Europe -- Continued
Austria

219	General works
220	Militia
221.A-Z	By region or province, A-Z

Belgium

222	General works
223	Militia
224.A-Z	By region or province, A-Z

Denmark

225	General works
226	Militia
227.A-Z	By region or province, A-Z

France

228	General works
229	Militia
230.A-Z	By region or province, A-Z

Germany
Including West Germany

231	General works
232	Militia
233.A-Z	By region or province, A-Z

East Germany

233.5	General works
233.52	Militia
233.53.A-Z	By region or province, A-Z

Great Britain

234	General works
235	Militia
236.A-Z	By region or province, A-Z

Greece

237	General works
238	Militia
239.A-Z	By region or province, A-Z

Netherlands

240	General works
241	Militia
242.A-Z	By region or province, A-Z

Italy

243	General works
244	Militia
245.A-Z	By region or province, A-Z

Norway

246	General works
247	Militia

	Tactics and regulations
	By region or country
	Europe
	Norway -- Continued
248.A-Z	By region or province, A-Z
	Portugal
249	General works
250	Militia
251.A-Z	By region or province, A-Z
	Russia. Soviet Union
252	General works
253	Militia
254.A-Z	By region or province, A-Z
	Spain
255	General works
256	Militia
257.A-Z	By region or province, A-Z
	Sweden
258	General works
259	Militia
260.A-Z	By region or province, A-Z
	Switzerland
261	General works
262	Militia
263.A-Z	By region or province, A-Z
	Turkey
264	General works
265	Militia
266.A-Z	By region or province, A-Z
269.A-Z	Other European countries, A-Z
	e.g.
269.P7	Poland
269.R8	Romania
269.Y8	Yugoslavia
	Asia
270	General works
	China
271	General works
272	Militia
273.A-Z	By region or province, A-Z
	India
274	General works
275	Militia
276.A-Z	By region or province, A-Z
	Japan
277	General works
278	Militia

	Field engineering -- Continued
390	Miscellaneous topics (not A-Z)
	Including rigging, block and tackle, etc.
	Cf. TJ1350+ Hoisting and conveying machinery
	Fortification
	General works
400	Early through 1800
401	1801-
403	Field fortification
	Trenches and trench warfare see UG446
	Permanent fortification
405	General works
405.15	Bunkers
405.2	City walls
	Cf. NA493+ Military architecture
407	Miscellaneous topics (not A-Z)
	Including wire entanglements
	Iron and steel for land defenses
	Including testing
408	General works
409.A-Z	Special systems, A-Z
409.G8	Gruson's
	Fortifications and defenses. By region or country
	United States
410	General works
411.A-Z	By region or state, A-Z
412.A-Z	By place, A-Z
	e.g.
412.K4	Key West
412.N3	Narragansett Bay
412.N5	New York (N.Y.)
412.P3	Panama Canal
412.S42	San Pedro (Calif.)
	Other regions or countries
	Canada
413	General works
414.A-Z	By region or province, A-Z
415.A-Z	By place, A-Z
	Mexico
416	General works
417.A-Z	By region or state, A-Z
418.A-Z	By place, A-Z
	Central America
419	General works
420.A-Z	By region or country, A-Z
421.A-Z	By place, A-Z
	West Indies

UG

	Attack and defense. Siege warfare
	Chemical warfare. Gas and flame
	Special gases, A-Z -- Continued
447.5.O74	Organophosphorus compounds
447.5.P5	Phenylimido-phosgene
447.6	Gas masks (Military use)
447.65	Incendiary weapons
447.7	Smoke screens. Smoke tactics
447.8	Biological warfare. Bacterial warfare
448	Coast defenses
	For coast defenses by place see UG410+
449	Camouflage
	Cf. V215 Marine camouflage
450	Military application of mechanical engineering
455	Military metrology
460	Military architecture and building
	Military geology
465	General works
	Military geophysics
465.3	General works
465.5	Military seismology
	For seismic verification of arms control, including nuclear arms control see UA12.5
467	Military meteorology
468	Military hydrology
	Military surveying, topography, and mapping
	Cf. GA125 Topographic drawing
	Cf. GA151 Map reading
	Cf. TA501+ General surveying
	Cf. TR900+ Industrial reproduction
	Cf. UA985+ Military geography
470	General works
	By region or country
472	United States
	e.g. United States. Army Map Service
473.A-Z	Other regions or countries, A-Z
474	Military sketching
475	Military surveillance
	Cf. UA12.5 Disarmament inspection and arms control and nuclear arms control verification
	Cf. UG1500+ Space surveillance
476	Military photography
478	Military aspects of automation
	Cf. V399 Automation in the naval sciences
478.5	Military use of automatic checkout equipment
479	Military uses of artificial intelligence

480	Military uses of electricity
	Cf. UG560+ Electricians
	Cf. UG590+ Military telegraphy and telephony
482	Military use of telemeter
485	Military use of electronics
486	Military use of lasers
486.5	Directed-energy weapons
487	Military use of infrared rays
488	Military uses of electrooptics and optoelectronics
489	Military use of information display systems
489.5	Military use of nanomaterials
490	Land mines. Mine fields. Mine countermeasures
	Cf. U428.S8 United States. School of Submarine Defense
	Cf. V856+ Submarine mines. Mine laying. Mine sweeping
	Technical troops and other special corps
	Technical troops
	Including military artificers
500	General works
	By region or country
	United States
503	General works
504.A-.W	By state, A-W
505.A-Z	Other regions or countries, A-Z
	Sappers. Bridge troops
510	General works
	By region or country
	United States
513	General works
514.A-.W	By state, A-W
515.A-Z	Other regions or countries, A-Z
	Railroad troops
	Cf. UG345 Railroads. Armored trains
520	General works
	By region or country
	United States
523	General works
524.A-.W	By state, A-W
525.A-Z	Other regions or countries, A-Z
	Pioneer troops
530	General works
	By region or country
	United States
533	General works
534.A-.W	By state, A-W
535.A-Z	Other regions or countries, A-Z

	Technical troops and other special corps -- Continued
	Mining and torpedo troops
	Cf. UG490 Land mines. Mine fields
	Cf. V856+ Submarine mines. Mine laying
550	General works
	By region or country
	United States
553	General works
554.A-.W	By state, A-W
555.A-Z	Other regions or countries, A-Z
	Electricians
	Cf. UG480 Military uses of electricity
	Cf. UG590+ Military telegraphy and telephony
560	General works
	By region or country
	United States
563	General works
564.A-.W	By state, A-W
565.A-Z	Other regions or countries, A-Z
	Military signaling
	Signal troops. Signal corps, etc.
570	General works
	By region or country
	United States
573	General works
574.A-.W	By state, A-W
575.A-Z	Other regions or countries, A-Z
580	General works on military signaling
582.A-Z	Special systems, A-Z
582.D6	Disc signaling
582.H2	Hand signaling
582.H4	Heligraph
582.P4	Panel signaling
582.S4	Semaphores
582.S68	Sound signaling
582.V5	Visual signaling
	Military telegraphy and telephony
	Including general telecommunication and wiring
	Cf. UA980 Telegraphic connections
590	General works
	By region or country
	United States
593	General works
594.A-.W	By state, A-W
595.A-Z	Other regions or countries, A-Z
	Military telegraphy and telegraph troops
600	General works

	Military telegraphy and telephony
	Military telegraphy and telegraph troops -- Continued
	By region or country
	United States
603	General works
604.A-.W	By state, A-W
605.A-Z	Other regions or countries, A-Z
607	Submarine cables
	Military telephony
610	General works
	By region or country
610.5.A-Z	Other regions or countries, A-Z
	Military radio
	Cf. VG76+ Naval wireless, radio
611	General works
	By region or country
611.3	United States
611.5.A-Z	Other regions or countries, A-Z
	Military radar
	Cf. UG1420+ Military aeronautics
612	General works
	By region or country
612.3	United States
612.5.A-Z	Other regions or countries, A-Z
	Military television
613	General works
	By region or country
613.3	United States
613.5.A-Z	Other regions or countries, A-Z
	Military electric lighting
	Including searchlights
614	General works
	By region or country
614.3	United States
614.5.A-Z	Other regions or countries, A-Z
	Military motor vehicles
	For motor transportation see UC340+
615	General works
	By region or country
	United States
618	General works
619.A-.W	By state, A-W
620.A-Z	Other regions or countries, A-Z

	Air forces. Air warfare
	Cf. KF7405+ Law of the United States
	Cf. TL500+ Aeronautics (Technology)
	Cf. U263 Atomic warfare
	Cf. UA926+ Civil defense
	Cf. UC330+ Air transportation
	Cf. UF767 Bombs
	Cf. VG90+ Naval aviation
622	Periodicals. Societies
623	Congresses
	Museums. Exhibitions
623.3.A1	General works
623.3.A2-Z	By region or country, A-Z

Under each country:

.x	General works
.x2A-.x2Z	Special. By city, A-Z

624	Collected works (nonserial)
	History
	For specific wars, see classes D-F
625	General works
	By country see UG633+
	Biography
	Cf. TL539+ Aeronautics
626	Collective
626.2.A-Z	Individual, A-Z
627	Addresses, essays, lectures
628	Dictionaries. Encyclopedias
630	General works
631	Juvenile works
632	General special
	Including international cooperation, psychological aspects
	Military air shows. Air tattoos. Military aeronautical
	competitions
632.2	General works
632.3.A-Z	By region or country, A-Z
	Soldiers' or airmens' handbooks
632.4	General works
	United States
632.43	General works
632.44.A-.W	By state, A-W
632.45.A-Z	Other regions or countries, A-Z
	By region or country
	United States
633	General works
633.2	Air Force expenditures and budgets. Accounting
634.A-.W	By state, A-W
	Air bases and airfields

	By region or country	
	United States	
	Air bases and airfields -- Continued	
634.49	General works	
634.5.A-Z	Special. By name, A-Z	
635.A-Z	Other regions or countries, A-Z	
	Under each country:	
	.x	*General works*
	.x2A-.x2Z	*Air bases and airfields. By name, A-Z*
	Education and training	
	Including flight training	
	Cf. TL710+ Aeronautics	
637	General works	
	By region or country	
	United States	
638	General works	
638.3.A-.W	By state, A-W	
	United States. Air Force Academy, Colorado Springs, Colo.	
(638.5.A1)	Act of incorporation	
	see KF7273+	
	Administration	
638.5.C3	Regulations	
638.5.C4	General orders	
638.5.C5	Conduct grades	
638.5.C7	Circulars	
638.5.C8	Memoranda	
638.5.E1	Annual report of Superintendent	
638.5.E3	Annual report of Inspectors	
638.5.E4	Annual report of Board of Visitors	
638.5.E45	Special reports, hearings, etc., of Board of Visitors	
638.5.E5	General congressional documents. By date	
638.5.E9	Documents relating to hazing. By date	
638.5.F3	Commencement orations	
638.5.F5	Miscellaneous addresses and speeches	
638.5.F7	Other documents, reports, etc.	
	Including semiofficial material	
638.5.F8	Special days and events. By date	
638.5.G3	Information for graduates	
638.5.H2	Rosters of officers, etc. (United States Air Force)	
	Registers	
638.5.H3	Official annual	
638.5.H4	Other official. By date	
	Nonofficial	
638.5.H5	Cullum's register	
638.5.H7-.H8	Other	

	Education and training
	By region or country
	United States
	United States. Air Force Academy, Colorado Springs, Colo. -- Continued
638.5.J1	Student publications. Annuals, etc.
	Graduate publications
638.5.K1	Reunions of graduates' associations
638.5.K3	Bulletins of graduates' associations
638.5.K5-.K7	Other
	General works on the academy. Histories
638.5.L1A1-.L1A5	Official works
638.5.L3	Illustrated works. Views
	Biography
	Cf. U410.H3+ Registers
638.5.M1A1-.M1A5	Collective
638.5.M1A6-.M1Z	Individual, A-Z
638.5.N1	Class histories. By date
638.5.P1	Descriptive works. Life at the Air Force Academy
638.5.Q1	Miscellaneous topics (not A-Z)
	e.g. How to get to the Air Force Academy
	Examination papers
638.5.R1	General works
638.5.R3	Entrance examinations
638.6.A-Z	Other schools. By place, A-Z
638.8	Reserve Officers' Training Corps (R.O.T.C.)
639.A-Z	Other regions or countries, A-Z
	Under each country:
	.x *General works*
	.x2A-.x2Z *Individual schools. By place, A-Z*
	Military aeronautical research
640	General works
	By region or country
	United States
643	General works
643.5.A-.W	By state, A-W
644.A-Z	Individual establishments. By place, A-Z
645.A-Z	Other regions or countries, A-Z
	Drill regulations
	Cf. U169 Drill manuals (all arms)
670	General works
	By region or country
	United States
673	General works
674.A-.W	By state, A-W
675.A-Z	Other regions or countries, A-Z

	Tactics
	Including bombing, strafing, dog fighting, air mining
	Cf. U260 Combined operations (Army, navy, air)
700	General works
	By region or country
	United States
703	General works
704.A-.W	By state, A-W
705.A-Z	Other regions or countries, A-Z
	Air defenses
	Cf. TH1097 Bombproof shelters. Fallout shelters
	Cf. UA926+ Civil defense
	Cf. UF625 Antiaircraft guns
730	General works
	By region or country
	United States
733	General works
734.A-.W	By state, A-W
735.A-Z	Other regions or countries, A-Z
	Ballistic missile defenses
	Cf. UG1312.A6 Antimissile missiles
	Cf. UG1530 Space warfare
740	General works
	By region or country
	United States
743	General works
744.A-.W	By state, A-W
745.A-Z	Other regions or countries, A-Z
	Aerial reconnaissance
	For reconnaissance satellites, space surveillance, see
	UG1500+
760	General works
	By region or country
	United States
763	General works
764.A-.W	By state, A-W
765.A-Z	Other regions or countries, A-Z
	Organization. Personnel management
770	General works
	By region or country
	United States
773	General works
774.A-.W	By state, A-W
775.A-Z	Other regions or countries, A-Z
	Officers
790	General works
	By region or country

	Organization. Personnel management
	Officers
	By region or country -- Continued
	United States
793	General works
794.A-.W	By state, A-W
795.A-Z	Other regions or countries, A-Z
	Noncommissioned officers. Airmen
	Cf. UD480+ Airborne troops
820	General works
	By region or country
	United States
823	General works
824.A-.W	By state, A-W
825.A-Z	Other regions or countries, A-Z
	Minorities, women, etc. in air forces
830	General works
	United States
833	General works
834.A-Z	Individual groups, A-Z
835.A-Z	Other regions or countries, A-Z
	Reserves. Air National Guard
850	General works
	By region or country
	United States
853	General works
854.A-.W	By state, A-W
855.A-Z	Other regions or countries, A-Z
	Recruiting, enlistment, etc.
880	General works
	By region or country
	United States
883	General works
884.A-.W	By state, A-W
885.A-Z	Other regions or countries, A-Z
	Records, accounting, etc.
910	General works
	By region or country
	United States
913	General works
914.A-.W	By state, A-W
915.A-Z	Other regions or countries, A-Z
	Pay, allowances, etc.
940	General works
	By region or country
	United States
943	General works

	Organization. Personnel management
	Pay, allowances, etc.
	By region or country
	United States -- Continued
944.A-.W	By state, A-W
945.A-Z	Other regions or countries, A-Z
	Furloughs, leave, etc.
970	General works
	By region or country
	United States
973	General works
974.A-.W	By state, A-W
975.A-Z	Other regions or countries, A-Z
	Rewards, brevets, decorations, medals, etc.
	Cf. UG1180+ Insignia, badges, etc. (Clothing and equipment of Air Force members)
976	General works
	United States
	For United States societies of medal winners see E181
977	General works
978.A-.W	By state, A-W
979.A-Z	Other regions or countries, A-Z
	Medical service
980	General works
	By region or country
	United States
983	General works
984.A-.W	By state, A-W
985.A-Z	Other regions or countries, A-Z
	Social work, recreation, etc.
990	General works
	By region or country
	United States
993	General works
994.A-.W	By state, A-W
995.A-Z	Other regions or countries, A-Z
	Chaplains. Chaplain's assistants
1000	General works
	By region or country
	United States
1003	General works
1004.A-.W	By state, A-W
1005.A-Z	Other regions or countries, A-Z
	Public relations. Press. War correspondents
1010	General works
	By region or country
	United States

	Organization. Personnel management
	Public relations. Press. War correspondents
	By region or country
	United States -- Continued
1013	General works
1014.A-.W	By state, A-W
1015.A-Z	Other regions or countries, A-Z
	Air force police
	Cf. UB820+ Military police
1020	General works
	By region or country
	United States
1023	General works
1024.A-.W	By state, A-W
1025.A-Z	Other regions or countries, A-Z
	Air force prisons
1040	General works
	By region or country
	United States
1043	General works
1044.A-.W	By state, A-W
1045.A-Z	Other regions or countries, A-Z
	Air bases
1097	General works
	By region or country see UG633+
	Equipment and supplies
1100	General works
	By region or country
	United States
1103	General works
1104.A-.W	By state, A-W
1105.A-Z	Other regions or countries, A-Z
	Procurement and contracts
1120	General works
	By region or country
	United States
1123	General works
1124.A-.W	By state, A-W
1125.A-Z	Other regions or countries, A-Z
	Personnel
1130	General works
	By region or country
	United States
1133	General works
1134.A-.W	By state, A-W
1135.A-Z	Other regions or countries, A-Z
	Barracks, quarters, etc.

	Equipment and supplies
	Personnel
	Barracks, quarters, etc. -- Continued
1140	General works
	By region or country
	United States
1143	General works
1144.A-.W	By state, A-W
1145.A-Z	Other regions or countries, A-Z
	Uniforms
1160	General works
	By region or country
	United States
1163	General works
1164.A-.W	By state, A-W
1165.A-Z	Other regions or countries, A-Z
	Equipment
1170	General works
	By region or country
	United States
1173	General works
1174.A-.W	By state, A-W
1175.A-Z	Other regions or countries, A-Z
	Insignia, badges, etc.
	Cf. UG976+ Rewards, brevets, decorations, medals, etc.
1180	General works
	By region or country
	United States
1183	General works
1184.A-.W	By state, A-W
1185.A-Z	Other regions or countries, A-Z
	Operational
1200	General works
	By region or country
	United States
1203	General works
1204.A-.W	By state, A-W
1205.A-Z	Other regions or countries, A-Z
	Airships
1220	General works
	By region or country
	United States
1223	General works
1224.A-.W	By state, A-W
1225.A-Z	Other regions or countries, A-Z
	Helicopters

	Equipment and supplies
	Operational
	Helicopters -- Continued
1230	General works
1232.A-Z	By type, A-Z
1232.A88	Attack helicopters
1232.O28	Observation helicopters
1232.S43	Search and rescue helicopters
1232.T72	Transport helicopters
	By region or country
	United States
1233	General works
1234.A-.W	By state, A-W
1235.A-Z	Other regions or countries, A-Z
	Airplanes
	Including instrumentation, recognition, camouflage
	For manufacture and testing see TL685.3
	For types of airplanes of particular countries see UG1243+
1240	General works
1242.A-Z	By type, A-Z
1242.A19	Aggressor aircraft
1242.A25	Antisubmarine aircraft
1242.A27	Army cooperation aircraft. Combat liaison airplanes
1242.A28	Attack planes
	Including dive bombers
1242.B6	Bombers
	Combat liaison airplanes see UG1242.A27
	Composite aircraft see UG1242.P53
1242.D7	Drone aircraft
1242.E43	Electronic warfare aircraft
1242.F5	Fighter planes
1242.G85	Gunships
1242.P53	Piggyback aircraft. Composite aircraft
1242.R4	Reconnaissance airplanes
1242.S73	Stealth aircraft
1242.T36	Tanker planes
1242.T67	Trainer planes
1242.T7	Transport planes
	Unmanned aerial vehicles see UG1242.D7
1242.V47	Vertically rising aircraft (V/STOL aircraft)
	By region or country
	United States
1243	General works
1244.A-.W	By state, A-W
1245.A-Z	Other regions or countries, A-Z

Equipment and supplies
Operational -- Continued
Ordnance
For manufacture see UF530+

1270	General works
1272.A-Z	By type, A-Z
1272.B65	Bombsights

By region or country
United States

1273	General works
1274.A-.W	By state, A-W
1275.A-Z	Other regions or countries, A-Z

Bombs
For types of bombs of particular countries see UG1282.A+

1280	General works
1282.A-Z	By type, A-Z
1282.A8	Atomic

Including hydrogen bombs
Cf. U264+ Atomic weapons

1282.C45	Cluster
1282.F7	Fragmentation
1282.G8	Guided
1282.I6	Incendiary
1282.N48	Neutron

Cf. U264+ Atomic weapons
By region or country
United States

1283	General works
1284.A-.W	By state, A-W
1285.A-Z	Other regions or countries, A-Z

Missiles and rockets
For manufacture see UF530+
For types of missiles and rockets of particular countries see UG1312.A+

1310	General works
1312.A-Z	By type, A-Z
1312.A35	Air-to-air
1312.A6	Antimissile

Cf. UG740+ Ballistic missile defenses

1312.A63	Antiship
1312.A8	Atomic
1312.B34	Ballistic
1312.C7	Cruise
1312.I2	ICBM
1312.M2	MIRV
1312.S87	Surface-to-air missiles

	Equipment and supplies
	Operational
	Missiles and rockets
	By type, A-Z -- Continued
1312.S88	Surface-to-surface missiles
	By region or country
	United States
1313	General works
1314.A-.W	By state, A-W
1315.A-Z	Other regions or countries, A-Z
	Aircraft guns and small arms
	For manufacture see UF530+
1340	General works
	By region or country
	United States
1343	General works
1344.A-.W	By state, A-W
1345.A-Z	Other regions or countries, A-Z
	Balloons and kites
1370	General works
	By region or country
	United States
1373	General works
1374.A-.W	By state, A-W
1375.A-Z	Other regions or countries, A-Z
	Air force vehicles
1400	General works
	By region or country
	United States
1403	General works
1404.A-.W	By state, A-W
1405.A-Z	Other regions or countries, A-Z
	Radar and electronics in military aeronautics. Electric installations of air forces
1420	General works
	By region or country
	United States
1423	General works
1424.A-.W	By state, A-W
1425.A-Z	Other region or countries, A-Z
	Infrared rays in military aeronautics
1430	General works
	By region or country
	United States
1434.A-.W	By state, A-W
1435.A-.W	Other regions or countries, A-Z

	Military astronautics. Space warfare. Space surveillance
	Cf. UA12.5 Nuclear arms control verification
	Cf. UG1310+ Missiles and rockets
1500	Periodicals. Societies. Serials
1505	Congresses
1509	Dictionaries and encyclopedias
1515	History
1520	General works
	By region or country
1523	United States
1525.A-Z	Other regions or countries, A-Z
1530	Space warfare. Interplanetary warfare
	Cf. UG740+ Ballistic missile defenses

	Other services
	Chaplains. Chaplain's assistants. Chapel managers
20	General works
	By region or country
	United States
23	General works
24.A-Z	By region or state, A-Z
25.A-Z	Other regions or countries, A-Z
	Cyclists
	For motorcycles see UC347
30	General works
	By region or country
	United States
33	General works
34.A-Z	By region or state, A-Z
35.A-Z	Other regions or countries, A-Z
	Bands
	For military music, see class M
40	General works
	By region or country
	United States
43	General works
44.A-Z	By region or state, A-Z
45.A-Z	Other regions or countries, A-Z
	Banks and banking services
60	General works
	By region or country
	United States
63	General works
64.A-Z	By region or state, A-Z
65.A-Z	Other regions or countries, A-Z
70	Orderlies. Dispatch carriers
	Postal service
80	General works
	By region or country
	United States
83	General works
84.A-Z	By region or state, A-Z
85.A-Z	Other regions or countries, A-Z
	Use of animals in military service
87	General works
90	Pigeons for military communications
	For World War II see D810.P53
100	Dogs for military communications, etc.
100.5.A-Z	Other, A-Z
100.5.B38	Bats
100.5.B67	Bottlenose dolphins

	Use of animals in military service	
	Other, A-Z -- Continued	
100.5.E44	Elephants	
	Medical and sanitary service	
201	Periodicals. Societies	
205	Congresses	
	Museums. Exhibitions	
206.A1	General works	
206.A2-Z	By region or country	

Under each country:

.x	General works
.x2A-.x2Z	Special. By city, A-Z

	History, statistics, etc.
215	General works
	By region or country
	Including description, organization, and administration
221	America
222	North America
	United States
	Official publications
223.A1-.A29	Serial
223.A3-.A39	Separate. By date
223.A4-.A49	Statistics
223.A5	Nonofficial statistics
223.A6-.Z5	Other nonofficial works
224	By period

For accounts of medical and sanitary services in a
  particular war, see the war in classes D-F
For World War I, 1914-1918 see D628+
For World War II, 1939-1945 see D806+
For Mexican War, 1846-1848 see E412.5
For Civil War, 1861-1865 see E621+
For Spanish-American War, 1898 see E731

225.A-Z	By region or state, A-Z
225.O3	Report of Surgeon General of Ohio
	Other regions or countries
226	Canada
227.5	Latin America (General)
228	Mexico
	Central America
230	General works
231.A-Z	By country, A-Z
	West Indies
232	General works
233.A-Z	By island or island group, A-Z
	South America
234	General works

Medical and sanitary service
History, statistics, etc.
By region or country
Other regions or countries
South America -- Continued

236	Argentina
238	Bolivia
241	Brazil
243	Chile
245	Colombia
247	Ecuador
	Guianas
249	General works
249.5	Suriname. Dutch Guiana
250	French Guiana
251	Paraguay
252	Peru
253	Uruguay
254	Venezuela
	Europe
255	General works
256	World War I
256.3	World War II
	Great Britain
257	General works
258.2	17th century
258.3	18th century
258.4	19th century
258.6	World War I
258.7	World War II
259	England and Wales
261	Scotland
263	Northern Ireland
265	Austria
267	Belgium
269	Denmark
271	France
	Germany
	Including West Germany
273	General works
273.1	Prussia
273.3	Bavaria
273.5	Saxony
273.7	Württemberg
274.5	East Germany
275	Greece
276.5	Ireland (Eire)

Medical and sanitary service
History, statistics, etc.
By region or country
Other regions or countries
Europe -- Continued
277   Netherlands
279   Italy
281   Norway
283   Portugal
285   Russia. Soviet Union. Russia (Federation)
286.5   Scandinavia (General)
287   Spain
289   Sweden
291   Switzerland
Turkey see UH311
295.A-Z   Other European countries, A-Z
Asia
299   General works
301   China
303   India
305   Japan
307   Iran
311   Turkey
313.A-Z   Other Asian countries, A-Z
Africa
315   General works
317   Egypt
319.A-Z   Other African countries, A-Z
321   Australia
322.5   New Zealand
Pacific islands
323   General works
324.A-Z   By island or group of islands, A-Z
Biography
Including nurses
341   Collective
347.A-Z   Individual, A-Z
390   General works
United States
393   Official. By date
394   Nonofficial. By author
395.A-Z   Other regions or countries, A-Z
396   Soldiers' first-aid manuals
Army medical schools
By region or country
United States
398   General works

	Medical and sanitary service	
	Army medical schools	
	By region or country	
	United States -- Continued	
398.5.A-Z	By region or state, A-Z	
	Under each state:	
	.x	*General works*
	.x2A-.x2Z	*Local, A-Z*
	.x3A-.x3Z	*Special schools. By name, A-Z*
399.A-Z	Other regions or countries, A-Z	
	Under each country:	
	.x	*General works*
	.x2A-.x2Z	*Local, A-Z*
	.x3A-.x3Z	*Special schools. By name, A-Z*
	Research. Laboratories	
399.5	General works	
	By region or country	
399.6	United States	
399.7.A-Z	Other regions or countries, A-Z	
	Organization and service	
	Including surgeons, physicians, medical service	
400	General works	
	By region or country see UH221+	
	Manuals see UH390	
	Apothecary service	
420	General works	
	By region or country	
	United States	
423	General works	
424.A-Z	By region or state, A-Z	
425.A-Z	Other regions or countries, A-Z	
	Dental service	
430	General works	
	By region or country	
	United States	
433	General works	
434.A-Z	By region or state, A-Z	
435.A-Z	Other regions or countries, A-Z	
	Medical supplies. Surgical appliances	
440	General works	
	By region or country	
	United States	
443	General works	
444.A-Z	By region or state, A-Z	
445.A-Z	Other regions or countries, A-Z	
	Bacteriology. Vaccination, etc.	
450	General works	

UH

	Medical and sanitary service
	Organization and service
	Bacteriology. Vaccination, etc. -- Continued
	By region or country
	United States
453	General works
454.A-Z	By region or state, A-Z
455.A-Z	Other regions or countries, A-Z
	Hospital service
	For hospitals and hospital services in a particular war, see the war in classes D-F
	Cf. RA960+ Hospital administration, etc.
460	General works
	By region or country
	United States
463	General works
464.A-Z	By region or state, A-Z
465.A-Z	Other regions or countries, A-Z
	Hospitals. Buildings, equipment, etc.
	For administration see UH460+
470	General works
	By region or country
	United States
473	General works
474.A-Z	By region or state, A-Z
474.5.A-Z	Hospitals. By place, A-Z
	For World War I see D629.U7+
	For World War II see D807.U6+
475.A-Z	Other regions or countries, A-Z
	Drill regulations, etc.
480	General works
	By region or country
	United States
483	General works
484.A-Z	By region or state, A-Z
485.A-Z	Other regions or countries, A-Z
	Diet and cookery for sick soldiers
	Cf. RM219+ Dietary cookbooks including cookery and dietaries for the sick
	By region or country
487.A1-.A19	United States
487.A3-Z	Other regions or countries, A-Z
	Nurses and nursing
490	General works
	By region or country
	United States
493	General works

	Medical and sanitary service
	Nurses and nursing
	By region or country
	United States -- Continued
494.A-Z	By region or state, A-Z
495.A-Z	Other regions or countries, A-Z
	Transportation. Ambulances
500	General works
	By region or country
	United States
503	General works
504.A-Z	By region or state, A-Z
505.A-Z	Other regions or countries, A-Z
	Equipment of medical corps
510	General works
	By region or country
	United States
513	General works
514.A-Z	By region or state, A-Z
515.A-Z	Other regions or countries, A-Z
	Care of sick and wounded. Relief societies
	Cf. UH490+ Nurses and nursing
520	General works
	By region or country
	United States
523	General works
524.A-Z	By region or state, A-Z
525.A-Z	Other regions or countries, A-Z
534	International congresses. By date
	Red Cross
	For general documents and reports other than those of war see HV560+
535	General works
537.A-Z	National associations. By region or country, A-Z
	Other relief associations
	By region or country
543	United States
545.A-Z	Other regions or countries, A-Z
551	Service in individual wars (if not otherwise provided for)
	Prefer classification with individual wars in classes D-F
	For World War II see D808+
	For South African War see DT1890+
(560)	Employment for crippled soldiers and sailors
	see UB360+
570	Treatment of the dead
	Cf. UB397 Markers for soldiers' graves
	Military hygiene and sanitation

	Military hygiene and sanitation -- Continued
600	General works
601	Minor works
	By region or country
603	United States
605.A-Z	Other regions or countries, A-Z
611	Tropical hygiene
	Cf. RC960+ Tropical medicine
	Handbooks, manuals, etc.
623	English and American
625	Other (not A-Z)
627	Physiological research
	Including energy expenditure, etc.
	Mental hygiene, psychiatry, etc.
629	General works
	By region or country
629.3	United States
629.5.A-Z	Other regions or countries, A-Z
630	Protection of morals and health
	Including liquor problem, prostitution, venereal diseases, etc.
	Veterinary service
650	General works
	By region or country
653	United States
655.A-Z	Other regions or countries, A-Z
	Public relations. Press. War correspondents
700	General works
	By region or country
703	United States
705.A-Z	Other regions or countries, A-Z
	Civic actions. Nonmilitary use of armed forces for social and
	economic development
720	General works
	By region or country
723	United States
725.A-Z	Other regions or countries, A-Z
	Military unions. Union movements in armed forces
740	General works
	By region or country
743	United States
745.A-Z	Other regions or countries, A-Z
	Military social work. Social welfare services
750	General works
	By region or country
	United States
	Including Armed Forces
755	General works

	Military social work. Social welfare services
	By region or country
	United States -- Continued
760	Army
769.A-Z	Other regions or countries, A-Z
	Recreation and information services
	Cf. U327+ Military sports
	Cf. U715+ Nonmilitary education in armies
800	General works
	By region or country
	United States
	Including Armed Forces
805	General works
	Army
810	General works
815.A-Z	Local, A-Z
819.A-Z	Other regions or countries, A-Z
	Motion picture service
820	General works
	By region or country
	United States
	Including Armed Forces
825	General works
825.5	Film catalogs
826	Army
829.A-Z	Other regions or countries, A-Z
	Radiobroadcasting service
	Cf. PN6120.R2 Radio plays for programs
850	General works
	By region or country
	United States
	Including Armed Forces
855	General works
857	Army
859.A-Z	Other regions or countries, A-Z
	Off-post recreation
	Including civilian sponsored recreation (community organizations, etc.)
900	General works
	By region or country
905	United States
910.A-Z	Other regions or countries, A-Z

	Naval science (General)
	Periodicals and societies. By language of publication
1	English
2	French
3	German
4	Italian
5	Other languages (not A-Z)
7	Congresses
9	Almanacs, etc. (Official)
	Cf. V11.A+ Navy lists
(10)	Yearbooks (Nonofficial)
	see V1+
11.A-Z	Navy lists. Official yearbooks. By region or country, A-Z
	Class with administrative documents in VA, if annual report of department is included
	Museums. Exhibitions
13.A1	General works
13.A2-Z	By region or country, A-Z

Under each country:

.x	General works
.x2A-.x2Z	Special. By city, A-Z

	United States
13.U5	General works
13.U6A-.U6Z	Individual museums. By city, A-Z
	Collected works (nonserial)
15	Several authors
17	Individual authors
19	Addresses, essays, lectures
21	General special
	Dictionaries and encyclopedias
	Including nautical dictionaries
23	General
24	Dictionaries in two or more languages
	History and antiquities of naval science
	Including history of navies and naval wars, naval policy, etc., in general
	For naval history, wars, and battles of individual countries, see classes D-F
	Cf. V720+ Antiquities of naval life
25	Philosophy of history
	Including theory of sea power
27	General works
	By period
	Ancient history
29	General works
33	Egyptians
35	Phoenicians. Carthaginians

	History and antiquities of naval science
	By period
	Ancient history -- Continued
37	Greeks
39	Romans
41	Other special
	Medieval history to 1492/1600
43	General works
45	Vikings
46	Other special
	Modern history
47	17th-18th centuries
51	19th century
53	20th century
55.A-Z	By region or country, A-Z
	Biography
	For military personnel identified with military events in the history of a particular country, see classes D-F
61	Collective
	By region or country
	United States
62	Collective
63.A-Z	Individual, A-Z
64.A-Z	Other regions or countries, A-Z
	Under each country:
	.x *Collective*
	.x2A-.x2Z *Individual, A-Z*
	Navy clubs. By region or country
	Cf. U56+ Army and navy clubs
66	United States
67.A-Z	Other American, A-Z
68	Great Britain
69.A-Z	Other regions or countries, A-Z
	General works
101	Early through 1800
103	1801-
105	General special
107	Popular works
109	Juvenile works
	Sailors' handbooks
	Cf. VD150+ Manuals for naval personnel
110	General works
	By navy
113	United States
115.A-Z	Other countries, A-Z
	Petty officers' handbooks
120	General works

310	Salutes. Honors. Ceremonies
	Cf. U350+ Military ceremonies
	Safety education and measures in navies
380	General works
	By region or country
	United States
383	General works
384.A-.W	By state, A-W
385.A-Z	Other regions or countries, A-Z
386	Protection and decontamination in atomic, biological, and chemical warfare. ABC defense
	Naval research
390	General works
	By region or country
	United States
393	General works
393.5.A-.W	By state, A-W
394.A-Z	Special establishments. By name, A-Z
395.A-Z	Other regions or countries, A-Z
	Military oceanography
	Cf. VK588+ Marine hydrography
396	General works
	By region or country
	United States
396.3	General works
396.4.A-Z	Special establishments. By place, A-Z
396.5.A-Z	Other regions or countries, A-Z
398	Data processing in the naval sciences
399	Automation in the naval sciences
	Cf. VK560+ Electronics in navigation
	Cf. VM480+ Shipborne electronic equipment
	Naval education
400	General works
	History
401	General works
	By period
402	Ancient
403	Medieval
	Modern
404	General works
405	Through 1800
407	19th century
409	20th century
	By region or country
	United States
411	General works
	United States. Naval Academy, Annapolis

	Naval education
	By region or country
	United States
	United States. Naval Academy, Annapolis -- Continued
415	General works
(415.A1)	Act of incorporation
	see KF7353.55
	Administration
	Regulations
415.C3	Serial
415.C32	Monographs. By date
	Special
415.C35	Routine and orders. By date
415.C4	Regulations for admission
415.C6	Regulations for appointment of cadet engineers
415.E1	Annual report of Superintendent
415.E3	Annual report of Inspectors
415.E4	Annual report of Board of Visitors
415.E5	General congressional documents. By date
415.E9	Documents relating to hazing. By date
415.F3A-.F3Z	Commencement orations. By speaker, A-Z
415.F5A-.F5Z	Miscellaneous addresses and speeches. By speaker, A-Z
415.F7	Other documents, reports, etc.
	Including semiofficial material
	Registers
415.H3-.H39	Official annual
415.H5	Other
	Student publications
415.J1A-.J1Z	Annuals. By name of publication, A-Z
	e.g.
415.J1L9	The Lucky Bag
415.J5A-.J5Z	Other serials. By name of publication, A-Z
415.J7	Miscellaneous
	Graduate publications
415.K1	Reunions of graduates
415.K3	Bulletins
415.K4	Class histories. By date
	Registers see V415.H5
415.L1	History and general works on the Naval Academy
415.L3	Illustrated works. Views
415.M1	Biography (not registers)
415.P1	Descriptive works. "Life at Annapolis"
415.Q1	Other miscellaneous
	Including how to gain admission into Annapolis
	Examination papers
415.R1	General works

	Naval education
	By region or country
	United States
	United States. Naval Academy, Annapolis
	Examination papers -- Continued
415.R3-.R39	Entrance examinations
415.R4	Mental examinations. By date
420	United States. Naval War College
425.A-Z	Other government schools, A-Z
	United States. School of Submarine Defense, Fort Totten, N.Y. see U428.S8
426	United States. Naval Reserve Officers' Training Corps
	Cf. VA80+ United States naval militia, naval reserves, etc.
427	V-12 program
	Private naval schools
430.A3	General works
430.A4-Z	Individual schools. By name, A-Z
	Naval training stations
433	General works
434.A-Z	By place, A-Z
	e.g.
434.G7	Great Lakes, Ill.
434.H2	Hampton Roads, Va.
	Training ships. Naval apprentices
435	General works
436.A-Z	By name, A-Z
437	United States Coast Guard (Revenue-Cutter Service) training
	Including appointment of cadets; United States Coast Guard Academy; etc.
	Cf. HJ6645+ Customs administration by the United States Coast Guard
438	Confederate States
	Canada
440	General works
441	General special
442.A-Z	Special subjects, A-Z
443.A-Z	Provinces, regions, etc., A-Z
444.A-Z	Schools, A-Z
	Mexico
445	General works
446	General special
447.A-Z	Special subjects, A-Z
448.A-Z	Provinces, regions, etc., A-Z
449.A-Z	Schools, A-Z
	Central America

Naval education
By region or country
Central America -- Continued
450   General works
453.A-Z   By region or country, A-Z
                   Under each country:
                     .x   *General works*
                     .x2A-.x2Z   *Schools. By place A-Z*
                 West Indies
455   General works
458.A-Z   By island or group of islands, A-Z
                   Under each:
                     .x   *General works*
                     .x2A-.x2Z   *Schools. By place, A-Z*
                 South America
465   General works
                 Argentina
466   General works
467   General special
468.A-Z   Schools, A-Z
                 Brazil
472   General works
473   General special
474.A-Z   Schools, A-Z
                 Chile
475   General works
476   General special
477.A-Z   Schools, A-Z
                 Colombia
478   General works
479   General special
480.A-Z   Schools, A-Z
                 Ecuador
481   General works
482   General special
483.A-Z   Schools, A-Z
                 Guyana
484   General works
484.2   General special
484.3.A-Z   Schools, A-Z
                 Suriname
485   General works
485.2   General special
485.3.A-Z   Schools, A-Z
                 French Guiana
486   General works
486.2   General special

Naval education
By region or country
Europe
Great Britain
Engineering and dockyard schools -- Continued
525.R1 Miscellaneous
530 Private naval schools
Austria
550 General works
551 General special
552.A-Z Special subjects, A-Z
553.A-Z Local, A-Z
554.A-Z Schools, A-Z
554.5.A-Z Training ships. By name, A-Z
For general works on training ships see V551
Belgium
555 General works
556 General special
557.A-Z Special subjects, A-Z
558.A-Z Local, A-Z
559.A-Z Schools, A-Z
Denmark
560 General works
561 General special
562.A-Z Special subjects, A-Z
563.A-Z Local, A-Z
564.A-Z Schools, A-Z
France
565 General works
566 General special
567.A-Z Special subjects, A-Z
568.A-Z Local, A-Z
569.A-Z Schools, A-Z
Germany
Including West Germany
570 General works
571 General special
572.A-Z Special subjects, A-Z
573.A-Z Local, A-Z
574.A-Z Schools, A-Z
East Germany
574.51 General works
574.52 General special
574.53.A-Z Special subjects, A-Z
574.54.A-Z Local, A-Z
574.55.A-Z Schools, A-Z
Greece

Naval education
  By region or country
    Europe
      Greece -- Continued

575	General works
576	General special
577.A-Z	Special subjects, A-Z
578.A-Z	Local, A-Z
579.A-Z	Schools, A-Z

      Netherlands

580	General works
581	General special
582.A-Z	Special subjects, A-Z
583.A-Z	Local, A-Z
584.A-Z	Schools, A-Z

      Italy

585	General works
586	General special
587.A-Z	Special subjects, A-Z
588.A-Z	Local, A-Z
589.A-Z	Schools, A-Z

      Norway

590	General works
591	General special
592.A-Z	Special subjects, A-Z
593.A-Z	Local, A-Z
594.A-Z	Schools, A-Z

      Portugal

595	General works
596	General special
597.A-Z	Special subjects, A-Z
598.A-Z	Local, A-Z
599.A-Z	Schools, A-Z

      Russia

600	General works
601	General special
602.A-Z	Special subjects, A-Z
603.A-Z	Local, A-Z
604.A-Z	Schools, A-Z

      Spain

605	General works
606	General special
607.A-Z	Special subjects, A-Z
608.A-Z	Local, A-Z
609.A-Z	Schools, A-Z

      Sweden

610	General works

	Naval education
	By region or country
	Europe
	Sweden -- Continued
611	General special
612.A-Z	Special subjects, A-Z
613.A-Z	Local, A-Z
614.A-Z	Schools, A-Z
	Turkey
	see V650.T9
	Balkan States
620	General works
621	Bulgaria
622	Romania
	Turkey see V650.T9
623.A-Z	Other European countries, A-Z
	Asia
625	General works
	China
630	General works
631	General special
632.A-Z	Special subjects, A-Z
633.A-Z	Local, A-Z
634.A-Z	Schools, A-Z
	India
635	General works
636	General special
637.A-Z	Special subjects, A-Z
638.A-Z	Local, A-Z
639.A-Z	Schools, A-Z
	Japan
640	General works
641	General special
642.A-Z	Special subjects, A-Z
643.A-Z	Local, A-Z
644.A-Z	Schools, A-Z
	Iran
645	General works
646	General special
647.A-Z	Special subjects, A-Z
648.A-Z	Local, A-Z
649.A-Z	Schools, A-Z
650.A-650.Z	Other Asian countries, A-Z
	e.g.
650.T9	Turkey
	Africa
660	General works

	Naval education
	By region or country
	Africa -- Continued
	Egypt
675	General works
676	General special
677.A-Z	Special subjects, A-Z
678.A-Z	Local, A-Z
679.A-Z	Schools, A-Z
680.A-Z	Other African countries, A-Z
	Australia
690	General works
691	General special
692.A-Z	Special subjects, A-Z
693.A-Z	Local, A-Z
694.A-Z	Schools, A-Z
	New Zealand
694.1	General works
694.2	General special
694.3.A-Z	Special subjects, A-Z
694.4.A-Z	Local, A-Z
694.5.A-Z	Schools, A-Z
695.A-Z	Pacific Islands, A-Z
	General education. Nonnaval education
	Including education in subjects other than naval science
697	General works
	By region or country
698	United States
699.A-Z	Other regions or countries, A-Z
	Naval observations in special wars
	see classes D-F
(701)	To 1789
(703)	Napoleonic wars, 1789-1815
(705)	United States Civil War, 1861-1865
(707)	Franco-German War, 1870-1871
(709)	Spanish-American War, 1898
(713)	Russo-Japanese War, 1904-1905
(715)	World War I, 1914-1918
(716)	World War II, 1939-1945
	Naval life, manners and customs, antiquities, etc.
	Cf. G549 Life aboard men-of-war
	Cf. PN6231.M5 Anecdotes, facetiae, satire, etc.
	Cf. V25+ Antiquities of naval science
720	General works
	By period
725	Ancient
	Medieval

	Naval life, manners and customs, antiquities, etc.
	By period
	Medieval -- Continued
730	General works
733	General special
	Modern
735	General works
736	American
737	English
738	French
739	German
740	Italian
741	Russian
742	Spanish
743.A-Z	Other, A-Z
745	Naval curiosities
	War vessels: Construction, armament, etc.
	For individual ships see VA10+
	Cf. VM1+ Naval architecture, shipbuilding, etc.
750	General works
	By period
755	Ancient
	Medieval
760	General works
763	General special
	Modern
765	General works
767	General special
	Construction (General)
795	To 1815/1830 (Period of sailing vessels)
797	1815/1830-1860 (Period of steam vessels)
799	1860-1900 (Period of armored vessels)
800	1901-
	Materials
805	General works
	By region or country
805.3	United States
805.5.A-805.5.Z	Other regions or countries, A-Z
810	Damage control
	Special types
	Battleships
815	General works
	By navy
815.3	United States
815.5.A-Z	Other countries, A-Z
	Cruisers
820	General works

	War vessels: Construction, armament, etc.
	Special types
	Cruisers -- Continued
	By navy
820.3	United States
820.5.A-Z	Other countries, A-Z
	Destroyers
825	General works
	By navy
825.3	United States
825.5.A-Z	Other countries, A-Z
	Frigates
826	General works
	By navy
826.3	United States
826.5.A-Z	Other countries, A-Z
	Fireships
827	General works
	By navy
827.3	United States
827.5.A-Z	Other countries, A-Z
	Torpedo boats
830	General works
	By navy
833	United States
835.A-Z	Other countries, A-Z
	Torpedo boat service
837	General works
838	Engineers, etc.
840	Torpedo boat destroyers
	Torpedos
	Including apparatus for projection, etc.
850	General works
855.A-Z	Special, A-Z
855.G7	Graydon aerial torpedo thrower
855.H3	Harvey sea torpedo
855.L4	Lay movable torpedo
855.W5	Whitehead torpedo
	Submarine mines. Minelaying. Minesweeping
	Cf. UG490 Landmines
	Cf. V210+ Submarine warfare
	Cf. VM479 Degaussing
856	General works
856.5.A-Z	By region or country, A-Z
	Submarine boats. Submarine forces
	Cf. V210+ Submarine warfare
	Cf. VM365+ Construction

V

	Navies: Organization, distribution, naval situation
10	General works
	Naval expenditures. Cost of navies
20	General works
	Budgets
25	General works
	By region or country
	see VA60+
	Navies of the world
40	General works
41	Popular works
42	Pictorial works
	Organization of naval militia, reserves, etc.
45	General works
	By region or country
	see VA80+
	Mobilization
48	General works
	By region or country
	see VA77+
	Naval situation, organization, etc.
	By region or country
	United States
	Naval situation, policy, etc. (General)
49	Periodicals. Societies
50	General works
	United States. Navy
	Cf. E182 Naval history
	Documents (General)
	Navy Department
	Cf. VA60 Naval expenditures and budgets
52.A1-.A19	General works
52.A2-.A29	Secretary of the Navy
52.A6-.A67	Bureau of Navigation. Bureau of Naval Personnel
52.A68-.A69	Office of Naval Material
52.A7-.A79	Office of Naval Operations
52.A8-.A89	Naval Consulting Board
	Bureau of Construction and Repair, Bureau of Ships see VM23
	Bureau of Engineering see VM623.A1+
	Bureau of Equipment see VC25+
	Bureau of Ordnance see VF23
	Bureau of Supplies and Accounts see VC35+
	Bureau of Yards and Docks see VM23
	List of officers see V11.A+
	Congressional documents, nonofficial reports, etc.

	Naval situation, organization, etc.
	By region or country
	United States
	United States. Navy
	Congressional documents, nonofficial reports, etc. -- Continued
53.A1-.A69	Compilations
	Cf. KF16+ Law of the United States
53.A7	Special
	By date
53.A8-Z	Nonofficial reports, statements, etc. to the Congress or its committees
54	Speeches
55	General works
	By period
56	Early works through 1860
57	1861-1880
58	1881-1970
58.4	1971-
59	Pictorial works
60	Naval expenditures and budgets. Accounting
61	Lists of vessels
	Distribution, etc.
62	General works
	Naval districts
62.5	General works
62.7	Special. By number
63.A-Z	Squadrons, fleets, etc. By name, A-Z
	e.g.
63.A8	Asiatic region
63.A83	Atlantic Fleet
63.N8	North Atlantic Squadron
63.P28	Patrol Squadron Two
65.A-Z	Ships. By name, A-Z
	e.g.
	For training ships see V436.A+
65.C3	California (Battleship)
65.C7	Constitution (Frigate)
65.D6	Dolphin (Steam dispatch boat)
65.F3	Fargo (Cruiser)
65.F7	Franklin D. Roosevelt (Aircraft carrier)
65.M2	Maine (Battleship)
65.M5	Merrimac (Frigate)
65.O6	Olympia (Cruiser)
65.V4	Vestal (Repair ship)
65.V6	Von Steuben (Transport ship)

VA

	Naval situation, organization, etc.
	By region or country
	United States
	United States. Navy
	Distribution, etc. -- Continued
66.A-Z	Other units. By name, A-Z
	Construction Battalions
66.C615	Maintenance Units. By number
66.C62	Mobile Construction Battalions. By number
	Naval ports, bases, reservations, docks, etc.
67	General works
68.A-Z	By place, A-Z
	Navy yards. Naval stations
	Cf. VA73+ Coaling stations, etc.
69	General works
70.A-Z	By place, A-Z
	Under each:
	.xA2-.xA7 Documents
	.xA8-.xZ Other
70.N5	New London, Conn. Naval Station
70.N7	Norfolk, Va. Navy Yard
	Now known as the Norfolk Naval Shipyard, Portsmouth, Va.
70.P5	Philadelphia. Navy Yard
	Now known as the Philadelphia Naval Shipyard, League Island, Pa.
70.P8	Portsmouth, N.H. Navy Yard
	Coaling stations, etc.
73	General works
74.A-Z	By place, A-Z
74.C4	Chiriqui, Panama
77	Mobilization
79	United States. Naval Auxiliary Service
	Including colliers, service craft, supply vessels, transports, etc.
	United States. Naval militia, naval reserves, etc.
80	General works
	By state
	Alabama
90	General history
91	Official publications (General)
92	Registers, lists, rosters
	Regulations and orders see VB15+
	Special organizations
93	By number
	e. g. 1st (Naval batallion)

Naval situation, organization, etc.
  By region or country
    United States
      United States. Naval militia, naval reserves, etc.
      By state
        Alabama
          Special organizations -- Continued

94.A-Z	By name, A-Z
95.A-Z	Ships. By name, A-Z
97	Miscellaneous topics (not A-Z)

        Alaska

98	General history
98.2	Official publications (General)
98.3	Registers, lists, rosters

          Regulations and orders see VB15+
          Special organizations

98.4	By number
	e. g. 1st (Naval battalion)
98.5.A-Z	By name, A-Z
98.6.A-Z	Ships. By name, A-Z
98.7	Miscellaneous topics (not A-Z)

        California

100	General history
101	Official publications (General)
102	Registers, lists, rosters

          Regulations and orders see VB15+
          Special organizations

103	By number
	e. g. 1st (Naval batallion)
104.A-Z	By name, A-Z
105.A-Z	Ships. By name, A-Z
107	Miscellaneous topics (not A-Z)

        Connecticut

110	General history
111	Official publications (General)
112	Registers, lists, rosters

          Regulations and orders see VB15+
          Special organizations

113	By number
	e. g. 1st (Naval batallion)
114.A-Z	By name, A-Z
115.A-Z	Ships. By name, A-Z
117	Miscellaneous topics (not A-Z)

        Delaware

120	General history
121	Official publications (General)

VA

Naval situation, organization, etc.
By region or country
United States
United States. Naval militia, naval reserves, etc.
By state
Delaware -- Continued
122 Registers, lists, rosters
Regulations and orders see VB15+
Special organizations
123 By number
e. g. 1st (Naval batallion)
124.A-Z By name, A-Z
125.A-Z Ships. By name, A-Z
127 Miscellaneous topics (not A-Z)
District of Columbia
130 General history
131 Official publications (General)
132 Registers, lists, rosters
Regulations and orders see VB15+
Special organizations
133 By number
e. g. 1st (Naval batallion)
134.A-Z By name, A-Z
135.A-Z Ships. By name, A-Z
137 Miscellaneous topics (not A-Z)
Florida
140 General history
141 Official publications (General)
142 Registers, lists, rosters
Regulations and orders see VB15+
Special organizations
143 By number
e. g. 1st (Naval batallion)
144.A-Z By name, A-Z
145.A-Z Ships. By name, A-Z
147 Miscellaneous topics (not A-Z)
Georgia
150 General history
151 Official publications (General)
152 Registers, lists, rosters
Regulations and orders see VB15+
Special organizations
153 By number
e. g. 1st (Naval batallion)
154.A-Z By name, A-Z
155.A-Z Ships. By name, A-Z

Naval situation, organization, etc.
By region or country
United States
United States. Naval militia, naval reserves, etc.
By state
Georgia -- Continued
157 Miscellaneous topics (not A-Z)
Hawaii
158 General history
158.2 Official publications (General)
158.3 Registers, lists, rosters
Regulations and orders see VB15+
Special organizations
158.4 By number
e. g. 1st (Naval batallion)
158.5.A-Z By name, A-Z
158.6.A-Z Ships. By name, A-Z
158.7 Miscellaneous topics (not A-Z)
Illinois
160 General history
161 Official publications (General)
162 Registers, lists, rosters
Regulations and orders see VB15+
Special organizations
163 By number
e. g. 1st (Naval batallion)
164.A-Z By name, A-Z
165.A-Z Ships. By name, A-Z
167 Miscellaneous topics (not A-Z)
Indiana
170 General history
171 Official publications (General)
172 Registers, lists, rosters
Regulations and orders see VB15+
Special organizations
173 By number
e. g. 1st (Naval batallion)
174.A-Z By name, A-Z
175.A-Z Ships. By name, A-Z
177 Miscellaneous topics (not A-Z)
Louisiana
180 General history
181 Official publications (General)
182 Registers, lists, rosters
Regulations and orders see VB15+
Special organizations

Naval situation, organization, etc.
   By region or country
     United States
      United States. Naval militia, naval reserves, etc.
       By state
        Louisiana
         Special organizations -- Continued

183	By number
	e. g. 1st (Naval batallion)
184.A-Z	By name, A-Z
185.A-Z	Ships. By name, A-Z
187	Miscellaneous topics (not A-Z)
	Maine
190	General history
191	Official publications (General)
192	Registers, lists, rosters
	Regulations and orders see VB15+
	Special organizations
193	By number
	e. g. 1st (Naval batallion)
194.A-Z	By name, A-Z
195.A-Z	Ships. By name, A-Z
197	Miscellaneous topics (not A-Z)
	Maryland
200	General history
201	Official publications (General)
202	Registers, lists, rosters
	Regulations and orders see VB15+
	Special organizations
203	By number
	e. g. 1st (Naval batallion)
204.A-Z	By name, A-Z
205.A-Z	Ships. By name, A-Z
207	Miscellaneous topics (not A-Z)
	Massachusetts
210	General history
211	Official publications (General)
212	Registers, lists, rosters
	Regulations and orders see VB15+
	Special organizations
213	By number
	e. g. 1st (Naval batallion)
214.A-Z	By name, A-Z
215.A-Z	Ships. By name, A-Z
217	Miscellaneous topics (not A-Z)
	Michigan

Naval situation, organization, etc.
  By region or country
    United States
      United States. Naval militia, naval reserves, etc.
        By state
          Michigan -- Continued

220	General history
221	Official publications (General)
222	Registers, lists, rosters
	Regulations and orders see VB15+
	Special organizations
223	By number
	e. g. 1st (Naval batallion)
224.A-Z	By name, A-Z
225.A-Z	Ships. By name, A-Z
227	Miscellaneous topics (not A-Z)
	Minnesota
230	General history
231	Official publications (General)
232	Registers, lists, rosters
	Regulations and orders see VB15+
	Special organizations
233	By number
	e. g. 1st (Naval batallion)
234.A-Z	By name, A-Z
235.A-Z	Ships. By name, A-Z
237	Miscellaneous topics (not A-Z)
	Mississippi
240	General history
241	Official publications (General)
242	Registers, lists, rosters
	Regulations and orders see VB15+
	Special organizations
243	By number
	e. g. 1st (Naval batallion)
244.A-Z	By name, A-Z
245.A-Z	Ships. By name, A-Z
247	Miscellaneous topics (not A-Z)
	Missouri
250	General history
251	Official publications (General)
252	Registers, lists, rosters
	Regulations and orders see VB15+
	Special organizations
253	By number
	e. g. 1st (Naval batallion)

Naval situation, organization, etc.
By region or country
United States
United States. Naval militia, naval reserves, etc.
By state
Missouri
Special organizations -- Continued
254.A-Z   By name, A-Z
255.A-Z   Ships. By name, A-Z
257   Miscellaneous topics (not A-Z)
New Hampshire
260   General history
261   Official publications (General)
262   Registers, lists, rosters
Regulations and orders see VB15+
Special organizations
263   By number
e. g. 1st (Naval batallion)
264.A-Z   By name, A-Z
265.A-Z   Ships. By name, A-Z
267   Miscellaneous topics (not A-Z)
New Jersey
270   General history
271   Official publications (General)
272   Registers, lists, rosters
Regulations and orders see VB15+
Special organizations
273   By number
e. g. 1st (Naval batallion)
274.A-Z   By name, A-Z
275.A-Z   Ships. By name, A-Z
277   Miscellaneous topics (not A-Z)
New York
280   General history
281   Official publications (General)
282   Registers, lists, rosters
Regulations and orders see VB15+
Special organizations
283   By number
e. g. 1st (Naval batallion)
284.A-Z   By name, A-Z
285.A-Z   Ships. By name, A-Z
287   Miscellaneous topics (not A-Z)
North Carolina
290   General history
291   Official publications (General)

Naval situation, organization, etc.
By region or country
United States
United States. Naval militia, naval reserves, etc.
By state
North Carolina -- Continued

292	Registers, lists, rosters
	Regulations and orders see VB15+
	Special organizations
293	By number
	e. g. 1st (Naval batallion)
294.A-Z	By name, A-Z
295.A-Z	Ships. By name, A-Z
297	Miscellaneous topics (not A-Z)
	Ohio
300	General history
301	Official publications (General)
302	Registers, lists, rosters
	Regulations and orders see VB15+
	Special organizations
303	By number
	e. g. 1st (Naval batallion)
304.A-Z	By name, A-Z
305.A-Z	Ships. By name, A-Z
307	Miscellaneous topics (not A-Z)
	Oregon
310	General history
311	Official publications (General)
312	Registers, lists, rosters
	Regulations and orders see VB15+
	Special organizations
313	By number
	e. g. 1st (Naval batallion)
314.A-Z	By name, A-Z
315.A-Z	Ships. By name, A-Z
317	Miscellaneous topics (not A-Z)
	Pennsylvania
320	General history
321	Official publications (General)
322	Registers, lists, rosters
	Regulations and orders see VB15+
	Special organizations
323	By number
	e. g. 1st (Naval batallion)
324.A-Z	By name, A-Z
325.A-Z	Ships. By name, A-Z

VA

Naval situation, organization, etc.
By region or country
United States
United States. Naval militia, naval reserves, etc.
By state
Pennsylvania -- Continued
327 Miscellaneous topics (not A-Z)
Rhode Island
330 General history
331 Official publications (General)
332 Registers, lists, rosters
Regulations and orders see VB15+
Special organizations
333 By number
e. g. 1st (Naval batallion)
334.A-Z By name, A-Z
335.A-Z Ships. By name, A-Z
337 Miscellaneous topics (not A-Z)
South Carolina
340 General history
341 Official publications (General)
342 Registers, lists, rosters
Regulations and orders see VB15+
Special organizations
343 By number
e. g. 1st (Naval batallion)
344.A-Z By name, A-Z
345.A-Z Ships. By name, A-Z
347 Miscellaneous topics (not A-Z)
Texas
350 General history
351 Official publications (General)
352 Registers, lists, rosters
Regulations and orders see VB15+
Special organizations
353 By number
e. g. 1st (Naval batallion)
354.A-Z By name, A-Z
355.A-Z Ships. By name, A-Z
357 Miscellaneous topics (not A-Z)
Vermont
359 General history
359.2 Official publications (General)
359.3 Registers, lists, rosters
Regulations and orders see VB15+
Special organizations

Naval situation, organization, etc.

By region or country

United States

United States. Naval militia, naval reserves, etc.

By state

Vermont

Special organizations -- Continued

359.4	By number
	e. g. 1st (Naval batallion)
359.5.A-Z	By name, A-Z
359.6.A-Z	Ships. By name, A-Z
359.7	Miscellaneous topics (not A-Z)

Virginia

360	General history
361	Official publications (General)
362	Registers, lists, rosters
	Regulations and orders see VB15+
	Special organizations
363	By number
	e. g. 1st (Naval batallion)
364.A-Z	By name, A-Z
365.A-Z	Ships. By name, A-Z
367	Miscellaneous topics (not A-Z)

Washington

370	General history
371	Official publications (General)
372	Registers, lists, rosters
	Regulations and orders see VB15+
	Special organizations
373	By number
	e. g. 1st (Naval batallion)
374.A-Z	By name, A-Z
375.A-Z	Ships. By name, A-Z
377	Miscellaneous topics (not A-Z)

Wisconsin

380	General history
381	Official publications (General)
382	Registers, lists, rosters
	Regulations and orders see VB15+
	Special organizations
383	By number
	e. g. 1st (Naval batallion)
384.A-Z	By name, A-Z
385.A-Z	Ships. By name, A-Z
387	Miscellaneous topics (not A-Z)

VA

	Naval situation, organization, etc.
	By region or country
	United States
	United States. Naval militia, naval reserves, etc. -- Continued
390.A-Z	Organizations not localized. By name, A-Z
	Including United States. Coast Guard Reserve. Women's Reserve. "SPARS"; United States. Naval Reserve. Women's Reserve. "WAVES"
	Confederate States Navy
393	General works
395.A-Z	Navy yards, A-Z
	Canada
400	General works
400.5.A-Z	Ships. By name, A-Z
401.A-Z	By province, etc., A-Z
402	Naval militia
402.5	Latin America
	Mexico
403	General works
403.5.A-Z	Ships. By name, A-Z
404.A-Z	By province, etc., A-Z
405	Naval militia
	Central America
406	General works
407.A-Z	By region or country, A-Z
	West Indies
409	General works
410.A-Z	By island or group of islands, A-Z
	South America
415	General works
	Argentina
416	General works
416.5.A-Z	Ships. By name, A-Z
417.A-Z	By province, etc., A-Z
418	Naval militia
	Bolivia
419	General works
419.5.A-Z	Ships. By name, A-Z
420.A-Z	By province, etc., A-Z
421	Naval militia
	Brazil
422	General works
422.5.A-Z	Ships. By name, A-Z
423.A-Z	By province, etc., A-Z
424	Naval militia

Naval situation, organization, etc.
By region or country
South America -- Continued
Chile

425	General works
425.5.A-Z	Ships. By name, A-Z
426.A-Z	By province, etc., A-Z
427	Naval militia

Colombia

428	General works
428.5.A-Z	Ships. By name, A-Z
429.A-Z	By province, etc., A-Z
430	Naval militia

Ecuador

431	General works
431.5.A-Z	Ships. By name, A-Z
432.A-Z	By province, etc., A-Z
433	Naval militia
434	Guyana
435	Suriname
436	French Guiana

Paraguay

436.5	General works
436.55.A-Z	Ships. By name, A-Z
436.6.A-Z	By province, etc., A-Z
436.7	Naval militia

Peru

437	General works
437.5.A-Z	Ships. By name, A-Z
438.A-Z	By province, etc., A-Z
439	Naval militia

Uruguay

440	General works
440.5.A-Z	Ships. By name, A-Z
441.A-Z	By province, etc., A-Z
442	Naval militia

Venezuela

443	General works
443.5.A-Z	Ships. By name, A-Z
444.A-Z	By province, etc., A-Z
445	Naval militia

Europe
For naval affairs in NATO as a whole see UA646.3+

450	General works
	Great Britain
452	Periodicals. Societies

Naval situation, organization, etc.
  By region or country
    Europe
      Great Britain -- Continued

453	Documents (General)
454	General works
455	Naval expenditures. Estimates, budgets, etc.
456	Lists of vessels
457.A-Z	Squadrons, fleets, etc. By name, A-Z
458.A-Z	Ships. By name, A-Z
	e.g.
458.H6	Hood (Battle cruiser)
458.P4	Pembroke (Man-of-war)
458.5.A-Z	Other units. By name, A-Z
459	Naval ports, bases, etc.
459.A1	General works
459.A3-Z	By place, A-Z
459.S5	Singapore. Naval Base
	Navy yards. Naval stations
460.A1	General works
460.A3-Z	By place, A-Z
	Coaling stations, wharves, docks, etc.
461.A1	General works
461.A3-Z	By place, A-Z
463	Mobilization
	Naval militia and reserves
464	General works
465.A-Z	By organization, A-Z
	By region or country
466	Scotland
467	Ireland
	Austria
470	Periodicals. Societies
471	Expenditures, budgets, etc.
472	Documents (General)
473.A1-.A49	Lists of vessels
473.A5-Z	General works
474.A-Z	Squadrons, fleets, etc. By name, A-Z
475.A-Z	Ships. By name, A-Z
	Including battleships, cruisers, submarines, etc.
	Naval ports and bases. Navy yards
476.A1	General works
476.A3-Z	By place, A-Z
	Coaling stations, wharves, docks, etc.
477.A1	General works
477.A3-Z	By place, A-Z

Naval situation, organization, etc.
By region or country
Europe
Austria -- Continued

478	Mobilization
479	Naval militia and reserves
	Belgium
480	Periodicals. Societies
481	Expenditures, budgets, etc.
482	Documents (General)
483.A1-.A49	Lists of vessels
483.A5-Z	General works
484.A-Z	Squadrons, fleets, etc. By name, A-Z
485.A-Z	Ships. By name, A-Z
	Including battleships, cruisers, submarines, etc.
	Naval ports and bases. Navy yards
486.A1	General works
486.A3-Z	By place, A-Z
	Coaling stations, wharves, docks, etc.
487.A1	General works
487.A3-Z	By place, A-Z
488	Mobilization
489	Naval militia and reserves
	Denmark
490	Periodicals. Societies
491	Expenditures, budgets, etc.
492	Documents (General)
493.A1-.A49	Lists of vessels
493.A5-Z	General works
494.A-Z	Squadrons, fleets, etc. By name, A-Z
495.A-Z	Ships. By name, A-Z
	Including battleships, cruisers, submarines, etc.
	Naval ports and bases. Navy yards
496.A1	General works
496.A3-Z	By place, A-Z
	Coaling stations, wharves, docks, etc.
497.A1	General works
497.A3-Z	By place, A-Z
498	Mobilization
499	Naval militia and reserves
	France
500	Periodicals. Societies
501	Expenditures, budgets, etc.
502	Documents (General)
503.A1-.A49	Lists of vessels
503.A5-Z	General works

VA

VA

Naval situation, organization, etc.
By region or country
Europe
Italy -- Continued

542	Documents (General)
543.A1-.A49	Lists of vessels
543.A5-Z	General works
544.A-Z	Squadrons, fleets, etc. By name, A-Z
545.A-Z	Ships. By name, A-Z
	Including battleships, cruisers, submarines, etc.
	Naval ports and bases. Navy yards
546.A1	General works
546.A3-Z	By place, A-Z
	Coaling stations, wharves, docks, etc.
547.A1	General works
547.A3-Z	By place, A-Z
548	Mobilization
549	Naval militia and reserves
	Norway
550	Periodicals. Societies
551	Expenditures, budgets, etc.
552	Documents (General)
553.A1-.A49	Lists of vessels
553.A5-Z	General works
554.A-Z	Squadrons, fleets, etc. By name, A-Z
555.A-Z	Ships. By name, A-Z
	Including battleships, cruisers, submarines, etc.
	Naval ports and bases. Navy yards
556.A1	General works
556.A3-Z	By place, A-Z
	Coaling stations, wharves, docks, etc.
557.A1	General works
557.A3-Z	By place, A-Z
558	Mobilization
559	Naval militia and reserves
	Portugal
560	Periodicals. Societies
561	Expenditures, budgets, etc.
562	Documents (General)
563.A1-.A49	Lists of vessels
563.A5-Z	General works
564.A-Z	Squadrons, fleets, etc. By name, A-Z
565.A-Z	Ships. By name, A-Z
	Including battleships, cruisers, submarines, etc.
	Naval ports and bases. Navy yards
566.A1	General works

Naval situation, organization, etc.
  By region or country
    Europe
      Portugal
        Naval ports and bases. Navy yards -- Continued

566.A3-Z	By place, A-Z
	Coaling stations, wharves, docks, etc.
567.A1	General works
567.A3-Z	By place, A-Z
568	Mobilization
569	Naval militia and reserves
	Russia
570	Periodicals. Societies
571	Expenditures, budgets, etc.
572	Documents (General)
573.A1-.A49	Lists of vessels
573.A5-Z	General works
574.A-Z	Squadrons, fleets, etc. By name, A-Z
575.A-Z	Ships. By name, A-Z
	Including battleships, cruisers, submarines, etc.
	Naval ports and bases. Navy yards
576.A1	General works
576.A3-Z	By place, A-Z
	Coaling stations, wharves, docks, etc.
577.A1	General works
577.A3-Z	By place, A-Z
578	Mobilization
579	Naval militia and reserves
	Spain
580	Periodicals. Societies
581	Expenditures, budgets, etc.
582	Documents (General)
583.A1-.A49	Lists of vessels
583.A5-Z	General works
584.A-Z	Squadrons, fleets, etc. By name, A-Z
585.A-Z	Ships. By name, A-Z
	Including battleships, cruisers, submarines, etc.
	Naval ports and bases. Navy yards
586.A1	General works
586.A3-Z	By place, A-Z
	Coaling stations, wharves, docks, etc.
587.A1	General works
587.A3-Z	By place, A-Z
588	Mobilization
589	Naval militia and reserves
	Sweden

Naval situation, organization, etc.
　　By region or country
　　　Europe
　　　　Sweden -- Continued
590　　　　　　　Periodicals. Societies
591　　　　　　　Expenditures, budgets, etc.
592　　　　　　　Documents (General)
593.A1-.A49　　　Lists of vessels
593.A5-Z　　　　General works
594.A-Z　　　　　Squadrons, fleets, etc. By name, A-Z
595.A-Z　　　　　Ships. By name, A-Z
　　　　　　　　　Including battleships, cruisers, submarines, etc.
　　　　　　　　Naval ports and bases. Navy yards
596.A1　　　　　　General works
596.A3-Z　　　　　By place, A-Z
　　　　　　　　Coaling stations, wharves, docks, etc.
597.A1　　　　　　General works
597.A3-Z　　　　　By place, A-Z
598　　　　　　　Mobilization
599　　　　　　　Naval militia and reserves
(600-609)　　　　Turkey
　　　　　　　　　see VA667.T9
　　　　　　　Balkan States
610　　　　　　　General works
612　　　　　　　Bulgaria
615　　　　　　　Romania
617　　　　　　　Yugoslavia
619.A-Z　　　　　Other European countries, A-Z
　　　　　Asia
620　　　　　　General works
　　　　　　China
630　　　　　　　Periodicals. Societies
631　　　　　　　Expenditures, budgets, etc.
632　　　　　　　Documents (General)
633.A1-.A49　　　Lists of vessels
633.A5-Z　　　　General works
634.A-Z　　　　　Squadrons, fleets, etc. By name, A-Z
635.A-Z　　　　　Ships. By name, A-Z
　　　　　　　　　Including battleships, cruisers, submarines, etc.
　　　　　　　　Naval ports and bases. Navy yards
636.A1　　　　　　General works
636.A3-Z　　　　　By place, A-Z
　　　　　　　　Coaling stations, wharves, docks, etc.
637.A1　　　　　　General works
637.A3-Z　　　　　By place, A-Z
638　　　　　　　Mobilization

Naval situation, organization, etc.
    By region or country
      Asia
        China -- Continued

639	Naval militia and reserves
	India
640	Periodicals. Societies
641	Expenditures, budgets, etc.
642	Documents (General)
643.A1-.A49	Lists of vessels
643.A5-Z	General works
644.A-Z	Squadrons, fleets, etc. By name, A-Z
645.A-Z	Ships. By name, A-Z
	Including battleships, cruisers, submarines, etc.
	Naval ports and bases. Navy yards
646.A1	General works
646.A3-Z	By place, A-Z
	Coaling stations, wharves, docks, etc.
647.A1	General works
647.A3-Z	By place, A-Z
648	Mobilization
649	Naval militia and reserves
	Japan
650	Periodicals. Societies
651	Expenditures, budgets, etc.
652	Documents (General)
653.A1-.A49	Lists of vessels
653.A5-Z	General works
654.A-Z	Squadrons, fleets, etc. By name, A-Z
655.A-Z	Ships. By name, A-Z
	Including battleships, cruisers, submarines, etc.
	Naval ports and bases. Navy yards
656.A1	General works
656.A3-Z	By place, A-Z
	Coaling stations, wharves, docks, etc.
657.A1	General works
657.A3-Z	By place, A-Z
658	Mobilization
659	Naval militia and reserves
660	Iran
665	Thailand
667.A-Z	Other Asian countries, A-Z
667.T9	Turkey
	Africa
670	General works
680	Former British Africa

	Naval situation, organization, etc.
	By region or country
	Africa -- Continued
690	Egypt
700.A-Z	Other African countries, A-Z
	Australia
710	Periodicals. Societies
711	Expenditures, budgets, etc.
712	Documents (General)
713.A1-.A49	Lists of vessels
713.A5-Z	General works
714.A-Z	Squadrons, fleets, etc. By name, A-Z
715.A-Z	Ships. By name, A-Z
	Including battleships, cruisers, submarines, etc.
	Naval ports and bases. Navy yards
716.A1	General works
716.A3-Z	By place, A-Z
	Coaling stations, wharves ,docks, etc.
717.A1	General works
717.A3-Z	By place, A-Z
718	Mobilization
719	Naval militia and reserves
	New Zealand
720	Periodicals. Societies
721	Expenditures, budgets, etc.
722	Documents (General)
723.A1-.A49	Lists of vessels
723.A5-Z	General works
724.A-Z	Squadrons, fleets, etc. By name, A-Z
725.A-Z	Ships. By name, A-Z
	Including battleships, cruisers, submarines, etc.
	Naval ports and bases. Navy yards
726.A1	General works
726.A3-Z	By place, A-Z
	Coaling stations, wharves, docks, etc.
727.A1	General works
727.A3-Z	By place, A-Z
728	Mobilization
729	Naval militia and reserves
	Pacific islands
730	General works
(740-749)	Hawaii
	see VA158+
750.A-Z	Other, A-Z

	By region or country
	South America -- Continued
50	French Guiana
51	Paraguay
52	Peru
53	Uruguay
54	Venezuela
	Europe
55	General works
	Great Britain
57	General works
59	England and Wales
61	Scotland
63	Northern Ireland
64.A-Z	Cities (or other special), A-Z
	Austria
65	General
66.A-Z	Subdivisions, A-Z
	Belgium
67	General
68.A-Z	Subdivisions, A-Z
	Denmark
69	General
70.A-Z	Subdivisions, A-Z
	France
71	General
72.A-Z	Subdivisions, A-Z
	Germany
73	General
74.A-Z	Subdivisions, A-Z
74.5	East Germany
	Greece
75	General
76.A-Z	Subdivisions, A-Z
76.5	Ireland (Éire)
	Netherlands
77	General
78.A-Z	Subdivisions, A-Z
	Italy
79	General
80.A-Z	Subdivisions, A-Z
	Norway
81	General
82.A-Z	Subdivisions, A-Z
	Portugal
83	General
84.A-Z	Subdivisions, A-Z

By region or country
Europe -- Continued
Russia in Europe
85	General
86.A-Z	Subdivisions, A-Z
86.5	Scandinavia (General)

Spain
87	General
88.A-Z	Subdivisions, A-Z

Sweden
89	General
90.A-Z	Subdivisions, A-Z

Switzerland
91	General
92.A-Z	Subdivisions, A-Z
	Turkey see VB111+
96.A-Z	Other European countries, A-Z

Asia
99	General works

China
101	General
102.A-Z	Subdivisions, A-Z

India
103	General
104.A-Z	Subdivisions, A-Z

Japan
105	General
106.A-Z	Subdivisions, A-Z

Iran
107	General
108.A-Z	Subdivisions, A-Z
	Russia in Asia. Siberia
109	General
110.A-Z	Subdivisions, A-Z

Turkey
111	General
112.A-Z	Subdivisions, A-Z
113.A-Z	Other Asian countries, A-Z

Africa
115	General works

Egypt
117	General
118.A-Z	Subdivisions, A-Z
119.A-Z	Other African countries, A-Z

Australia
121	General
122.A-Z	Subdivisions, A-Z

	By region or country -- Continued
122.5	New Zealand
	Pacific Islands
123	General works
124.A-Z	By island or group of islands, A-Z
	General works
144	Through 1800
145	1801-1970
146	1970-
160	Interior administration
	Including administration of fleets, stations, etc.
	Civil department
170	General works
	Civil employees
180	General works
	By region or country
183	United States
185.A-Z	Other regions or countries, A-Z
187.A-Z	Civil service examinations. By country, A-Z
190	Commanders, admirals, etc.
	Including duties, etc.
	Command of ships. Leadership
200	General works
200	General works
	By region or country
203	United States
205.A-Z	Other regions or countries, A-Z
210	Headquarters, aides, etc.
212	Naval command and control systems
	For military command and control systems see UB212
215	Operational readiness. Preparedness
	Class here general works on operational readiness
	For works on the readiness of a particular unit, such as a ship or
	a navy, see the number for the unit in subclass VA
	Inspection, inspectors, etc.
220	General works
	By region or country
223	United States
225.A-Z	Other regions or countries, A-Z
	Security measures for naval information
226	General works
	By region or country
227	United States
228.A-Z	Other regions or countries, A-Z

Security measures for naval information -- Continued
    Industrial security measures
        Cf. HV8290+ Private security services
        Cf. TH9701+ Burglar proof construction, alarm
           equipment, etc.

229	General works
	By region or country
229.3	United States
229.5.A-Z	Other regions or countries, A-Z

Intelligence
    Cf. V190 Reconnaissance
    Cf. VG1020 Photographic interpretation

230	General works
231.A-Z	By region or country, A-Z
240	Attachés
250	Espionage. Spies

Psychological warfare. Propaganda

252	General works
	By region or country
253	United States
254.A-Z	Other regions or countries, A-Z
255	Communications. Correspondence. Preparation of orders

    Cf. V270 Transmission of orders

Personnel management

257	General works
	By region or country
258	United States
258.5.A-Z	Other regions or countries, A-Z
259	Vocational guidance. The navy as a career. Job analysis

    For civil employees see VB170+

Enlisted personnel
    Including recruiting, enlistment, promotion, discharge, etc.
    For pay, allowances, etc. see VC50+

260	General works
	By region or country
	United States
263	General works
264.A-Z	By region or state, A-Z
265	Other regions or countries

Recruits
    Including medical, physical, and mental examination

270	General works
	By region or country
	United States
273	General works
274.A-Z	By region or state, A-Z
275.A-Z	Other regions or countries, A-Z

277	Demobilization. Civil employment
	Cf. UB356+ Provisions for veterans
(278)	Employment for disabled sailors
	see UB360+
	Pensions, disability benefits, bounties, prize money
280	General works
	By region or country
	United States
283	General works
284.A-Z	By region or state, A-Z
285	Other regions or countries
	Naval homes
	Cf. UB380+ Soldier's and sailors' homes
290	General works
	By region or country
	United States
293	General works
294.A-Z	By region or state, A-Z
295.A-Z	Other regions or countries, A-Z
	Naval cemeteries
300	General works
	By region or country
	United States
303	General works
304.A-Z	By region or state, A-Z
305.A-Z	Other regions or countries, A-Z
	Warrant officers. Petty officers, etc.
307	General works
	By region or country
308	United States
309.A-Z	Other regions or countries, A-Z
	Officers
	Including rank, grades, procurement, appointment, promotion,
	leaves of absence, retirement, etc.
	For pay, allowances, etc. see VC50+
310	General works
	By region or country
	United States
313	General works
314.A-Z	Individual cases, A-Z
	e.g.
314.G7	Admiral Goldsborough
314.H6	Admiral Hobson
315.A-Z	Other regions or countries, A-Z
	Minorities, women, etc. in navies
320	General works
	By region or country

	Minorities, women, etc. in navies
	By region or country -- Continued
	United States
323	General works
324.A-Z	Individual groups, A-Z
324.A47	African Americans
324.G38	Gays
324.W65	Women
325.A-Z	Other regions or countries, A-Z
	Rewards, brevets, medals of honor, badges, etc.
	Cf. VC345 Badges, insignia (Clothing and equipment of sailors)
330	General works
	By region or country
	United States
	For U.S. societies of medal winners see E181
333	General works
	Class here works on the Navy Blue Star (U.S. naval award) and the Navy Cross (U.S. decoration
334.A-Z	By region or state, A-Z
335.A-Z	Other regions or countries, A-Z
	Provision for widows and orphans
	Cf. HV3025+ Protection, assistance, and relief for mariners
340	General works
	By region or country
	United States
343	General works
344.A-Z	By region or state, A-Z
345.A-Z	Other regions or countries, A-Z
(350-955)	Naval law
	see class K
(350)	General works
(353)	International law
	By region or country
	United States
	see KF7345+
(360)	Naval law
(363)	Naval regulations
(365)	General orders
(368)	Regulations for naval militia and reserves
(369.A-.W)	Regulations for states, A-W
(369.5)	Laws and regulations for Confederate States
	Other regions or countries
(370-379)	Canada
(380-389)	Mexico
	Central America
(390)	General works

Naval law
  By region or country
    Other regions or countries
      Central America -- Continued

Naval law
  By region or country
    Other regions or countries
      Europe
        Other regions or countries -- Continued
(699.Y8)   Yugoslavia
      Asia
(700)   General works
(710-719)   China
(720-729)   India
(730-739)   Japan
(740.A-Z)   Other regions or countries, A-Z
(740.T9)   Turkey
      Africa
(750)   General works
(760)   Egypt
(770.A-Z)   Other regions or countries, A-Z
(775)   Australia
(777)   New Zealand
      Pacific Islands
(780)   General works
(785.A-Z)   By island or group of islands, A-Z
    Judiciary. Administration of naval justice
(790)   General works
      By region or country
(793)   United States
(795.A-Z)   Other regions or countries, A-Z
    Courts-martial
(800)   General works
      By region or country
(803)   United States
                see KF7646+
(805.A-Z)   Other regions or countries, A-Z
      Individual cases
(806)   United States
                see KF7646+
(807.A-Z)   Other regions or countries, A-Z
    Courts of inquiry
(810)   General works
      By region or country
        United States
            see KF7646+
(813)   General works
(814.A-Z)   Individual cases, A-Z
(815.A-Z)   Other regions or countries, A-Z
  Naval discipline
(840)   General works

	Naval discipline -- Continued
	By region or country
(843)	United States
(845.A-Z)	Other regions or countries, A-Z
	Naval crimes and misdemeanors
(850)	General works
	By region or country
(853)	United States
(855.A-Z)	Other regions or countries, A-Z
	Mutiny
(860)	General works
	By region or country
(863)	United States
(865.A-Z)	Other regions or countries, A-Z
(867.A-Z)	By vessel, A-Z
	Desertion
(870)	General works
	By region or country
(873)	United States
(875.A-Z)	Other regions or countries, A-Z
(880)	Other special (not A-Z)
	Includes looting
	Punishments. Prisons and prison ships. Prisoners
(890)	General works
	By region or country
(893)	United States
(895.A-Z)	Other regions or countries, A-Z
(910)	Corporal punishment. Flogging
	Shore patrol. Military police in navies
(920)	General works
	By region or country
(923)	United States
(925.A-Z)	Other regions or countries, A-Z
(955)	Miscellaneous topics (not A-Z)

	Naval maintenance
10	General works
	Organization of service
	United States
20	General works
	Bureau of Equipment (1862-1910)
25	Reports
26	Regulations, etc. By date
	Bureau of Supplies and Accounts (1892-
35	Reports
36	Regulations, etc. By date
	Other publications
38	Official. By date
39	Nonofficial
	Naval militia and reserves
40	General works
41	By region or state
	Pay Department. Pay, allowances, etc.
50	Serial reports
53	Regulations. By date
54	Pay and interest tables
60	Handbooks, manuals, etc.
61	Special reports, hearings, etc. By date
64	Nonofficial works
65	Miscellaneous topics (not A-Z)
	Other regions or countries
	Canada
90	Supplies
91	Pay and allowances
92	Naval militia and reserves
93.A-Z	By region or province, A-Z
	Mexico
94	Supplies
95	Pay and allowances
96	Naval militia and reserves
97.A-Z	By region or province, A-Z
	Central America
98	General works
99.A-Z	By region or country, A-Z
	West Indies
104	General works
105.A-Z	By island or group of islands, A-Z
	South America
110	General works
	Argentina
111	Supplies
112	Pay and allowances

VC

Organization of service
  Other regions or countries
    Europe
      Austria -- Continued

164	Supplies
165	Pay and allowances
166	Naval militia and reserves
167.A-Z	By region or province, A-Z

      Belgium

168	Supplies
169	Pay and allowances
170	Naval militia and reserves
171.A-Z	By region or province, A-Z

      Denmark

172	Supplies
173	Pay and allowances
174	Naval militia and reserves
175.A-Z	By region or province, A-Z

      France

176	Supplies
177	Pay and allowances
178	Naval militia and reserves
179.A-Z	By region or province, A-Z

      Germany

180	Supplies
181	Pay and allowances
182	Naval militia and reserves
183.A-Z	By region or province, A-Z

        East Germany

183.5	Supplies
183.51	Pay and allowances
183.52	Naval militia and reserves
183.53.A-Z	By region or province, A-Z

      Great Britain

184	Supplies
185	Pay and allowances
186	Naval militia and reserves
187.A-Z	By region or province, A-Z

      Greece

188	Supplies
189	Pay and allowances
190	Naval militia and reserves
191.A-Z	By region or province, A-Z

      Netherlands

192	Supplies
193	Pay and allowances
194	Naval militia and reserves

Organization of service
 Other regions or countries
  Europe
   Netherlands -- Continued
195.A-Z   By region or province, A-Z
   Italy
196   Supplies
197   Pay and allowances
198   Naval militia and reserves
199.A-Z   By region or province, A-Z
    Norway
200   Supplies
201   Pay and allowances
202   Naval militia and reserves
203.A-Z   By region or province, A-Z
    Portugal
204   Supplies
205   Pay and allowances
206   Naval militia and reserves
207.A-Z   By region or province, A-Z
    Russia
208   Supplies
209   Pay and allowances
210   Naval militia and reserves
211.A-Z   By region or province, A-Z
    Spain
212   Supplies
213   Pay and allowances
214   Naval militia and reserves
215.A-Z   By region or province, A-Z
    Sweden
216   Supplies
217   Pay and allowances
218   Naval militia and reserves
219.A-Z   By region or province, A-Z
    Turkey
       see VC245.T9
    Balkan States
224   General works
226   Bulgaria
228   Romania
229.A-Z   Other European regions or countries, A-Z
   Asia
230   General works
235   China
238   India
241   Japan

	Organization of service
	Other regions or countries
	Asia -- Continued
245.A-Z	Other Asian countries, A-Z
	e.g.
245.T9	Turkey
	Africa
247	General works
250	Egypt
253.A-Z	Other African regions or countries, A-Z
	Australia
255	General works
256.A-Z	By state, etc., A-Z
256.5	New Zealand
	Pacific Islands
257	General works
258.A-Z	By island or group of islands, A-Z
	Supplies and stores (General and personal)
	Including specifications, standards, controlled materials, surplus supplies, procurement, inspection, storekeeping, etc.
260	General works
	By region or country
	United States
263	General works
264.A-.W	By state, A-W
265.A-Z	Other regions or countries, A-Z
	Management methods
266	General works
266.5.A-Z	Special, A-Z
266.5.C7	Critical path analysis
266.5.E5	Electronic data processing
266.5.L5	Line of balance
	PERT see VC266.5.C7
267.A-Z	Contracts and claims. By country, A-Z
268.A-Z	Commandeering, compensation, etc. By country, A-Z
	Equipment of vessels, supplies, allowances, etc.
270	General works
	By region or country
	United States
273	General works
274.A-.W	By state, A-W
275.A-Z	Other regions or countries, A-Z
	Fuel
	Including supplies, costs, etc.
	For coaling stations, colliers and collier services of a particular country, see the country, e.g. VA73+ United States; VA461 Great Britain, etc.

VC

Equipment of vessels, supplies, allowances, etc.
Fuel -- Continued
276.A1   General works
276.A3-.A49   United States
                Cf. HD242.5 Naval oil reserves
276.A5-Z   Other regions or countries, A-Z
279.A-Z   Other supplies for vessels, A-Z
279.C3   Cables
279.H45   Hemp
279.R6   Rope
279.R8   Rubber
279.T5   Timber
279.T6   Tools
Clothing and equipment
280   General works
                By region or country
                United States
283   General works
284.A-.W   By state, A-W
285.A-Z   Other regions or countries, A-Z
Uniforms
300   General works
                By region or country
                United States
303   General works
304.A-.W   By state, A-W
305.A-Z   Other regions or countries, A-Z
307   Special purpose and protective clothing
                Including foul-weather gear
310   Shoes. Leggings. Footwear
                For care of feet, fitting shoes, etc. see UC490+
320   Headgear
330   Tailors. Tailoring
340   Accouterments
                Includes telescopes
345   Badges. Insignia
                Cf. VB330+ Rewards, brevets, medals of honor,
                    badges, etc.
Subsistence. Provisioning
350   General works
                By region or country
                United States
353   General works
354.A-.W   By state, A-W
355.A-Z   Other regions or countries, A-Z
Rations
360   General works

	Subsistence. Provisioning
	Rations -- Continued
	By region or country
	United States
363	General works
364.A-.W	By state, A-W
365.A-Z	Other regions or countries, A-Z
	Cookery. Messing
370	General works
	By region or country
	United States
373	General works
374.A-.W	By state, A-W
375.A-Z	Other regions or countries, A-Z
	Officers' clubs and messes
380	General works
	By region or country
	United States
383	General works
384.A-.W	By state, A-W
385.A-Z	Other regions or countries, A-Z
	Ship exchanges. Canteens
390	General works
	By region or country
	United States
393	General works
394.A-.W	By state, A-W
395.A-Z	Other regions or countries, A-Z
398	Galleys. Commissary equipment: Ranges, kitchen utensils, etc.
400	Refrigeration and refrigerating machinery
410	Water supply
	Including preservation, purification, etc.
	Cf. VM503+ Water supply on ships
	Navy yards and stations. Shore facilities
	Cf. VA67+ Distribution, etc.
412	General works
	By region or country
	United States
414	General works
415.A-.W	By state, A-W
416.A-Z	Other regions or countries, A-Z
417	Maintenance and repair
417.5	Sanitation. Refuse disposal, etc.
418	Electric power systems
	Barracks. Quarters. Housing
420	General works

	Navy yards and stations. Shore facilities
	Barracks. Quarters. Housing -- Continued
	By region or country
	United States
423	General works
424.A-.W	By state, A-W
425.A-Z	Other regions or countries, A-Z
430	Laundries. Laundering
	Including shipboard and shore-based facilities
	Ship records. Naval accounts and accounting
500	General works
	By region or country
	United States
503	General works
504.A-.W	By state, A-W
505.A-Z	Other regions or countries, A-Z
	Naval transportation
530	General works
	By region or country
	United States
533	General works
534.A-.W	By state, A-W
535.A-Z	Other regions or countries, A-Z
537	Packing and shipment of goods
	Transportation of personnel
550	General works
	By region or country
	United States
553	General works
554.A-.W	By state, A-W
555.A-Z	Other regions or countries, A-Z
	Automotive transportation. Motor transportation
570	General works
	By region or country
	United States
573	General works
574.A-.W	By state, A-W
575.A-Z	Other regions or countries, A-Z
580	Rail transportation
	Including technical works on railroads owned by the navy

	By region or country
	South America
	Colombia -- Continued
46.A-Z	Subdivisions, A-Z
	Ecuador
47	General works
48.A-Z	Subdivisions, A-Z
49	Guyana
49.5	Suriname
50	French Guiana
51	Paraguay
52	Peru
53	Uruguay
54	Venezuela
	Europe
55	General works
	Great Britain
57	General works
59	England and Wales
61	Scotland
63	Northern Ireland
64.A-Z	Cities (or other special), A-Z
	Austria
65	General works
66.A-Z	Subdivisions, A-Z
	Belgium
67	General works
68.A-Z	Subdivisions, A-Z
	Denmark
69	General works
70.A-Z	Subdivisions, A-Z
	France
71	General works
72.A-Z	Subdivisions, A-Z
	Germany
	Including West Germany
73	General works
74.A-Z	Subdivisions, A-Z
74.5	East Germany
	Greece
75	General works
76.A-Z	Subdivisions, A-Z
76.5	Ireland (Éire)
	Netherlands
77	General works
78.A-Z	Subdivisions, A-Z
	Italy

VD

VD

Drill regulations
By region or country
Europe
Austria -- Continued
221.A-Z   By province, etc., A-Z
Belgium
222   General works
223   Naval militia and reserves
224.A-Z   By province, etc., A-Z
Denmark
225   General works
226   Naval militia and reserves
227.A-Z   By province, etc., A-Z
France
228   General works
229   Naval militia and reserves
230.A-Z   By province, etc., A-Z
Germany
231   General works
232   Naval militia and reserves
233.A-Z   By province, etc., A-Z
Great Britain
234   General works
235   Naval militia and reserves
235.A-Z   By province, etc., A-Z
Greece
237   General works
238   Naval militia and reserves
239.A-Z   By province, etc., A-Z
Netherlands
240   General works
241   Naval militia and reserves
242.A-Z   By province, etc., A-Z
Italy
243   General works
244   Naval militia and reserves
245.A-Z   By province, etc., A-Z
Norway
246   General works
247   Naval militia and reserves
248.A-Z   By province, etc., A-Z
Portugal
249   General works
250   Naval militia and reserves
251.A-Z   By province, etc., A-Z
Russia
252   General works

Drill regulations
  By region or country
    Europe
      Russia -- Continued

253	Naval militia and reserves
254.A-Z	By province, etc., A-Z
	Spain
255	General works
256	Naval militia and reserves
257.A-Z	By province, etc., A-Z
	Sweden
258	General works
259	Naval militia and reserves
260.A-Z	By province, etc., A-Z
(264-266)	Turkey
	see VD280.T9
	Balkan States
267	General works
268.A-Z	By region or country, A-Z
269.A-Z	Other European countries, A-Z
	Asia
270	General works
	China
271	General works
272	Naval militia and reserves
273.A-Z	By province, etc., A-Z
	India
274	General works
275	Naval militia and reserves
276.A-Z	By province, etc., A-Z
	Japan
277	General works
278	Naval militia and reserves
279.A-Z	By province, etc., A-Z
280.A-Z	Other Asian countries, A-Z
	e.g.
280.T9	Turkey
	Africa
285	General works
	Egypt
286	General works
287	Naval militia and reserves
288.A-Z	By province, etc., A-Z
	Former British Africa
289	General works
290	Naval militia and reserves
291.A-Z	By country, A-Z

VE

By region or country
Other regions or countries
South America -- Continued

34	General works
	Argentina
36	General works
37.A-Z	Subdivisions, A-Z
	Bolivia
38	General works
39.A-Z	Subdivisions, A-Z
	Brazil
41	General works
42.A-Z	Subdivisions, A-Z
	Chile
43	General works
44.A-Z	Subdivisions, A-Z
	Colombia
45	General works
46.A-Z	Subdivisions, A-Z
	Ecuador
47	General works
48.A-Z	Subdivisions, A-Z
49	Guyana
49.5	Suriname
50	French Guiana
51	Paraguay
52	Peru
53	Uruguay
54	Venezuela
	Europe
55	General works
	Great Britain
57	General works
59	England and Wales
61	Scotland
63	Northern Ireland
64.A-Z	Cities (or other special), A-Z
	Austria
65	General works
66.A-Z	Subdivisions, A-Z
	Belgium
67	General works
68.A-Z	Subdivisions, A-Z
	Denmark
69	General works
70.A-Z	Subdivisions, A-Z
	France

	By region or country
	Other regions or countries
	Asia -- Continued
	India
103	General works
104.A-Z	Subdivisions, A-Z
	Japan
105	General works
106.A-Z	Subdivisions, A-Z
	Iran
107	General works
108.A-Z	Subdivisions, A-Z
	Russia in Asia. Siberia
109	General works
110.A-Z	Subdivisions, A-Z
	Turkey
111	General works
112.A-Z	Subdivisions, A-Z
113.A-Z	Other Asian countries, A-Z
	Africa
115	General works
	Egypt
117	General works
118.A-Z	Subdivisions, A-Z
119.A-Z	Other African countries, A-Z
	Australia
121	General works
122.A-Z	Subdivisions, A-Z
122.5	New Zealand
	Pacific islands
123	General works
124.A-Z	By island or group of islands, A-Z
	General works
144	Early works through 1800
145	1801-1970
146	1971-
	Handbooks, manuals, etc.
150	General works
	By region or country
153	United States
155.A-Z	Other regions or countries, A-Z
157	Tactics and maneuvers
	Drill regulations
	Including watch, station, quarter, and fire drills
	For watch duty in general see VK233
	By region or country
	United States

Drill regulations
By region or country
South America
Peru -- Continued
203   General works
204   Naval militia and reserves
205.A-Z   By province, etc., A-Z
Uruguay
206   General works
207   Naval militia and reserves
208.A-Z   By province, etc., A-Z
Venezuela
209   General works
210   Naval militia and reserves
211.A-Z   By province, etc., A-Z
Europe
215   General works
Austria
219   General works
220   Naval militia and reserves
221.A-Z   By province, etc., A-Z
Belgium
222   General works
223   Naval militia and reserves
224.A-Z   By province, etc., A-Z
Denmark
225   General works
226   Naval militia and reserves
227.A-Z   By province, etc., A-Z
France
228   General works
229   Naval militia and reserves
230.A-Z   By province, etc., A-Z
Germany
231   General works
232   Naval militia and reserves
233.A-Z   By province, etc., A-Z
Great Britain
234   General works
235   Naval militia and reserves
236.A-Z   By province, etc., A-Z
Greece
237   General works
238   Naval militia and reserves
239.A-Z   By province, etc., A-Z
Netherlands
240   General works

Drill regulations
  By region or country
    Europe
      Netherlands -- Continued

241	Naval militia and reserves
242.A-Z	By province, etc., A-Z
	Italy
243	General works
244	Naval militia and reserves
245.A-Z	By province, etc., A-Z
	Norway
246	General works
247	Naval militia and reserves
248.A-Z	By province, etc., A-Z
	Portugal
249	General works
250	Naval militia and reserves
251.A-Z	By province, etc., A-Z
	Russia
252	General works
253	Naval militia and reserves
254.A-Z	By province, etc., A-Z
	Spain
255	General works
256	Naval militia and reserves
257.A-Z	By province, etc., A-Z
	Sweden
258	General works
259	Naval militia and reserves
260.A-Z	By province, etc., A-Z
(264-266)	Turkey
	see VD280.T9
	Balkan States
267	General works
268.A-Z	By region or country, A-Z
269.A-Z	Other European countries, A-Z
	Asia
270	General works
	China
271	General works
272	Naval militia and reserves
273.A-Z	By province, etc., A-Z
	India
274	General works
275	Naval militia and reserves
276.A-Z	By province, etc., A-Z
	Japan

	Uniforms -- Continued
400	General works
	By region or country
403	United States
405.A-Z	Other regions or countries, A-Z
410	Shore service
	Cf. V175 Field service (General)
	Barracks, quarters, etc.
420	General works
	By region or country
	United States
422	General works
424.A-Z	By place, A-Z
425.A-Z	Other regions or countries, A-Z
	Training camps
430	General works
	By region or country
	United States
432	General works
434.A-Z	By place, A-Z
435.A-Z	Other regions or countries, A-Z
480	Records, accounting, etc.
490	Pay, allowances, etc.
	Rewards, brevets, medals of honor, badges, etc.
495	General works
	By region or country
495.3	United States
495.5.A-Z	Other regions or countries, A-Z
500	Miscellaneous topics (not A-Z)

VE

	Naval ordnance	
1	Periodicals. Societies	
	Museums. Exhibitions	
6.A1	General works	
6.A2-Z	By region or country	
	Under each country:	
	.x	*General works*
	.x2A-.x2Z	*Special. By city, A-Z*
7	Collected works (nonserial)	
15	History (General)	
	Including history of several countries	
	By region or country	
21	America	
	North America	
22	General works	
	United States	
23	General works	
23.7	Great Lakes	
24.A-.W	By state, A-W	
25.A-Z	By city, A-Z	
	Canada	
26	General works	
27.A-Z	Subdivisions, A-Z	
27.5	Latin America (General)	
	Mexico	
28	General works	
29.A-Z	Subdivisions, A-Z	
	Central America	
30	General works	
31.A-Z	By region or country, A-Z	
	West Indies	
32	General works	
33.A-Z	By island or group of islands, A-Z	
	South America	
34	General works	
	Argentina	
36	General works	
37.A-Z	Subdivisions, A-Z	
	Bolivia	
38	General works	
39.A-Z	Subdivisions, A-Z	
	Brazil	
41	General works	
42.A-Z	Subdivisions, A-Z	
	Chile	
43	General works	
44.A-Z	Subdivisions, A-Z	

<table>
<tr><td></td><td>By region or country</td></tr>
<tr><td></td><td>South America -- Continued</td></tr>
<tr><td></td><td>Colombia</td></tr>
<tr><td>45</td><td>General works</td></tr>
<tr><td>46.A-Z</td><td>Subdivisions, A-Z</td></tr>
<tr><td></td><td>Ecuador</td></tr>
<tr><td>47</td><td>General works</td></tr>
<tr><td>48.A-Z</td><td>Subdivisions, A-Z</td></tr>
<tr><td>49</td><td>Guyana</td></tr>
<tr><td>49.5</td><td>Suriname</td></tr>
<tr><td>50</td><td>French Guiana</td></tr>
<tr><td>51</td><td>Paraguay</td></tr>
<tr><td>52</td><td>Peru</td></tr>
<tr><td>53</td><td>Uruguay</td></tr>
<tr><td>54</td><td>Venezuela</td></tr>
<tr><td></td><td>Europe</td></tr>
<tr><td></td><td>Great Britain</td></tr>
<tr><td>55</td><td>General works</td></tr>
<tr><td>57</td><td>General works</td></tr>
<tr><td>59</td><td>England and Wales</td></tr>
<tr><td>61</td><td>Scotland</td></tr>
<tr><td>63</td><td>Northern Ireland</td></tr>
<tr><td>64.A-Z</td><td>Cities (or other special), A-Z</td></tr>
<tr><td></td><td>Austria</td></tr>
<tr><td>65</td><td>General works</td></tr>
<tr><td>66.A-Z</td><td>Subdivisions, A-Z</td></tr>
<tr><td></td><td>Belgium</td></tr>
<tr><td>67</td><td>General works</td></tr>
<tr><td>68.A-Z</td><td>Subdivisions, A-Z</td></tr>
<tr><td></td><td>Denmark</td></tr>
<tr><td>69</td><td>General works</td></tr>
<tr><td>70.A-Z</td><td>Subdivisions, A-Z</td></tr>
<tr><td></td><td>France</td></tr>
<tr><td>71</td><td>General works</td></tr>
<tr><td>72.A-Z</td><td>Subdivisions, A-Z</td></tr>
<tr><td></td><td>Germany</td></tr>
<tr><td></td><td>Including East Germany</td></tr>
<tr><td>73</td><td>General works</td></tr>
<tr><td>74.A-Z</td><td>Subdivisions, A-Z</td></tr>
<tr><td>74.5</td><td>East Germany</td></tr>
<tr><td></td><td>Greece</td></tr>
<tr><td>75</td><td>General works</td></tr>
<tr><td>76.A-Z</td><td>Subdivisions, A-Z</td></tr>
<tr><td>76.5</td><td>Ireland (Éire)</td></tr>
<tr><td></td><td>Netherlands</td></tr>
<tr><td>77</td><td>General works</td></tr>
<tr><td>78.A-Z</td><td>Subdivisions, A-Z</td></tr>
</table>

VF

	By region or country
	Europe -- Continued
	Italy
79	General works
80.A-Z	Subdivisions, A-Z
	Norway
81	General works
82.A-Z	Subdivisions, A-Z
	Portugal
83	General works
84.A-Z	Subdivisions, A-Z
	Russia in Europe
85	General works
86.A-Z	Subdivisions, A-Z
86.5	Scandinavia (General)
	Spain
87	General works
88.A-Z	Subdivisions, A-Z
	Sweden
89	General works
90.A-Z	Subdivisions, A-Z
	Switzerland
91	General works
92.A-Z	Subdivisions, A-Z
	Turkey see VF111+
96.A-Z	Other European countries, A-Z
	Asia
99	General works
	China
101	General works
102.A-Z	Subdivisions, A-Z
	India
103	General works
104.A-Z	Subdivisions, A-Z
	Japan
105	General works
106.A-Z	Subdivisions, A-Z
	Iran
107	General works
108.A-Z	Subdivisions, A-Z
	Russia in Asia. Siberia
109	General works
110.A-Z	Subdivisions, A-Z
	Turkey
111	General works
112.A-Z	Subdivisions, A-Z
113.A-Z	Other Asian countries, A-Z

Ordnance instructions and drill books
By region or country
South America -- Continued
175   General works
Argentina
176   General works
177   Naval militia and reserves
178.A-Z   By province, etc., A-Z
Brazil
182   General works
183   Naval militia and reserves
184.A-Z   By province, etc., A-Z
Chile
185   General works
186   Naval militia and reserves
187.A-Z   By province, etc., A-Z
Colombia
188   General works
189   Naval militia and reserves
190.A-Z   By province, etc., A-Z
Ecuador
191   General works
192   Naval militia and reserves
193.A-Z   By province, etc., A-Z
195   Guyana
196   Suriname
197   French Guiana
Peru
203   General works
204   Naval militia and reserves
205.A-Z   By province, etc., A-Z
Uruguay
206   General works
207   Naval militia and reserves
208.A-Z   By province, etc., A-Z
Venezuela
209   General works
210   Naval militia and reserves
211.A-Z   By province, etc., A-Z
Europe
215   General works
Austria
219   General works
220   Naval militia and reserves
221.A-Z   By province, etc., A-Z
Belgium
222   General works

Ordnance instructions and drill books
By region or country
Europe
Belgium -- Continued

223	Naval militia and reserves
224.A-Z	By province, etc., A-Z

Denmark

225	General works
226	Naval militia and reserves
227.A-Z	By province, etc., A-Z

France

228	General works
229	Naval militia and reserves
230.A-Z	By province, etc., A-Z

Germany

231	General works
232	Naval militia and reserves
233.A-Z	By province, etc., A-Z

Great Britain

234	General works
235	Naval militia and reserves
236.A-Z	By province, etc., A-Z

Greece

237	General works
238	Naval militia and reserves
239.A-Z	By province, etc., A-Z

Netherlands

240	General works
241	Naval militia and reserves
242.A-Z	By province, etc., A-Z

Italy

243	General works
244	Naval militia and reserves
245.A-Z	By province, etc., A-Z

Norway

246	General works
247	Naval militia and reserves
248.A-Z	By province, etc., A-Z

Portugal

249	General works
250	Naval militia and reserves
251.A-Z	By province, etc., A-Z

Russia

252	General works
253	Naval militia and reserves
254.A-Z	By province, etc., A-Z

Spain

Ordnance instructions and drill books
By region or country
Europe
Spain -- Continued
255 General works
256 Naval militia and reserves
257.A-Z By province, etc., A-Z
Sweden
258 General works
259 Naval militia and reserves
260.A-Z By province, etc., A-Z
(264-266) Turkey
see VF280.T9
Balkan States
267 General works
268.A-Z By region or country, A-Z
269.A-Z Other European countries, A-Z
Asia
270 General works
China
271 General works
272 Naval militia and reserves
273.A-Z By province, etc., A-Z
India
274 General works
275 Naval militia and reserves
276.A-Z By province, etc., A-Z
Japan
277 General works
278 Naval militia and reserves
279.A-Z By province, etc., A-Z
280.A-Z Other Asian countries, A-Z
e.g.
280.T9 Turkey
Africa
285 General works
Egypt
286 General works
287 Naval militia and reserves
288.A-Z By province, etc., A-Z
Former British Africa
289 General works
290 Naval militia and reserves
291.A-Z By country, A-Z
292.A-Z Other African countries, A-Z
Australia
295 General works

	Ordnance instructions and drill books
	By region or country
	Australia -- Continued
296	Naval militia and reserves
297.A-Z	By province, etc., A-Z
298	New Zealand
	Pacific islands
300	General works
302.A-Z	By island or group of islands, A-Z
	Target practice
310	General works
	By region or country
313	United States
315.A-Z	Other regions or countries, A-Z
	Equipment of naval artillery
320	General works
	By region or country
323	United States
325.A-Z	Other regions or countries, A-Z
	Shore service
	Cf. V175 Field service (General)
330	General works
	By region or country
333	United States
335.A-Z	Other regions or countries, A-Z
	Naval weapons systems
	Cf. V990+ Fleet missile weapons systems
346	General works
	By region or country
347	United States
348.A-Z	Other regions or countries, A-Z
	Ordnance and arms (General)
	Cf. UF520+ Military ordnance
350	General works
	By region or country
353	United States
355.A-Z	Other regions or countries, A-Z
357	Study and teaching
	Research
360	General works
	By region or country
360.3	United States
360.5.A-Z	Other countries or regions, A-Z
	Manufacture
370	General works
	By region or country
373	United States

VF

	Minor services of navies
	Chaplains. Chaplain's assistants. Religious program specialists
	Cf. UH20+ Military chaplains
20	General works
	By region or country
23	United States
25.A-Z	Other regions or countries, A-Z
	Bands
	For music see Class M
30	General works
	By region or country
33	United States
35.A-Z	Other regions or countries, A-Z
	Coast guard and coast signal service
50	General works
	By region or country
53	United States
	Cf. HJ6645+ Customs and administration
	Cf. V437 United States Coast Guard training
55.A-Z	Other regions or countries, A-Z
	Postal service
60	General works
	By region or country
63	United States
65.A-Z	Other regions or countries, A-Z
	Naval communication by telegraphy, telephone, etc.
	By telegraph
	Cf. UA980 Military telegraphic connections
70	General works
	By region or country
73	United States
75.A-Z	Other regions or countries, A-Z
	By wireless telegraph, radio, radar, etc.
	Cf. UG590+ Military radio, radar, etc.
	Cf. VK397 Marine signaling
	Cf. VK560+ Electronics in navigation
	Cf. VM480+ Shipborne electronic equipment and installations
76	General works
	By region or country
	United States
77.A1-.A5	Documents
77.A6-Z	General works
78.A-Z	Other regions or countries, A-Z
	By telephone
80	General works

Naval communication by telegraphy, telephone, etc.
By telephone -- Continued
By region or country
83   United States
85.A-Z   Other regions or countries, A-Z
Deception and diversion units
85.2   General works
By region or country
85.3   United States
85.5.A-Z   Other regions or countries, A-Z
Underwater demolition units
86   General works
By region or country
87   United States
Including United States. Navy. Underwater Demolition
Teams
88.A-Z   Other regions or countries, A-Z
Naval aviation. Air service. Air warfare
Cf. TL500+ Aeronautics (Technology)
Cf. UG622+ Military aeronautics
90   General works
By region or country
United States
93   General works
94.A-Z   By region or state, A-Z
94.5.A-Z   By station, field, etc., A-Z
e.g.
94.5.P4   Pensacola, Fla. Naval Air Station
94.6.A-Z   Organizations. By name, A-Z
94.7   Reserves
Including United States. Naval Air Reserve; United States.
Marine Air Reserve
95.A-Z   Other regions or countries, A-Z
Medical service
Including history, description, organization
For medical service in a particular war, see the war in classes D-F
Cf. R1+ Medicine
Cf. UH201+ Military medical service
100   Periodicals. Societies
103   Congresses
115   General works
By region or country
121   America
North America
122   General works
United States
123   General works

Medical service

By region or country

North America

United States -- Continued

123.5	Confederate States
123.7	Great Lakes
124.A-.W	By state, A-W
125.A-Z	By city, A-Z
	Canada
126	General
127.A-Z	Subdivisions, A-Z
127.5	Latin America (General)
	Mexico
128	General
129.A-Z	Subdivisions, A-Z
	Central America
130	General
131.A-Z	By region or country, A-Z
	West Indies
132	General
133.A-Z	By island or group of islands, A-Z
	South America
134	General works
	Argentina
136	General
137.A-Z	Subdivisions, A-Z
	Bolivia
138	General
139.A-Z	Subdivisions, A-Z
	Brazil
141	General
142.A-Z	Subdivisions, A-Z
	Chile
143	General
144.A-Z	Subdivisions, A-Z
	Colombia
145	General
146.A-Z	Subdivisions, A-Z
	Ecuador
147	General
148.A-Z	Subdivisions, A-Z
149	Guyana
149.5	Suriname
150	French Guiana
151	Paraguay
152	Peru
153	Uruguay

Medical service
By region or country
South America -- Continued

154	Venezuela
	Europe
155	General works
	Great Britain
157	General works
159	England and Wales
161	Scotland
163	Northern Ireland
164.A-Z	Cities (or other special), A-Z
	Austria
165	General
166.A-Z	Subdivisions, A-Z
	Belgium
167	General
168.A-Z	Subdivisions, A-Z
	Denmark
169	General
170.A-Z	Subdivisions, A-Z
	France
171	General
172.A-Z	Subdivisions, A-Z
	Germany
	Including West Germany
173	General
174.A-Z	Subdivisions, A-Z
174.5	East Germany
	Greece
175	General
176.A-Z	Subdivisions, A-Z
176.5	Ireland (Éire)
	Netherlands
177	General
178.A-Z	Subdivisions, A-Z
	Italy
179	General
180.A-Z	Subdivisions, A-Z
	Norway
181	General
182.A-Z	Subdivisions, A-Z
	Portugal
183	General
184.A-Z	Subdivisions, A-Z
	Russia in Europe
185	General

	Medical service
	By region or country
	Europe
	Russia in Europe -- Continued
186.A-Z	Subdivisions, A-Z
186.5	Scandinavia (General)
	Spain
187	General
188.A-Z	Subdivisions, A-Z
	Sweden
189	General
190.A-Z	Subdivisions, A-Z
	Switzerland
191	General
192.A-Z	Subdivisions, A-Z
	Turkey see VG211+
196.A-Z	Other European countries, A-Z
	Asia
199	General works
	China
201	General
202.A-Z	Subdivisions, A-Z
203-204	India
203	General
204.A-Z	Subdivisions, A-Z
	Japan
205	General
206.A-Z	Subdivisions, A-Z
	Iran
207	General
208.A-Z	Subdivisions, A-Z
	Russia in Asia. Siberia
209	General
210.A-Z	Subdivisions, A-Z
	Turkey
211	General
212.A-Z	Subdivisions, A-Z
213.A-Z	Other Asian countries, A-Z
	Africa
215	General works
	Egypt
217	General
218.A-Z	Subdivisions, A-Z
219.A-Z	Other African countries, A-Z
	Australia
221	General
222.A-Z	Subdivisions, A-Z

	Medical service
	By region or country -- Continued
222.5	New Zealand
	Pacific islands
223	General works
224.A-Z	By island or group of islands, A-Z
	Biography
	Including nurses
226	Collective
	Individual
	By region or country
227.A-Z	United States. By biographee, A-Z
228.A-Z	Other regions or countries, A-Z
	Study and teaching
230	General works
	By region or country
233	United States
235.A-Z	Other regions or countries, A-Z
	Research. Laboratories
240	General works
	By region or country
243	United States
245.A-Z	Other regions or countries, A-Z
	Surgeons
260	General works
	By region or country
263	United States
265.A-Z	Other regions or countries, A-Z
	Dispensaries
270	General works
	By region or country
273	United States
275.A-Z	Other regions or countries, A-Z
	Dental service
280	General works
	By region or country
283	United States
285.A-Z	Other regions or countries, A-Z
	Medical supplies. Surgical appliances
290	General works
	By region or country
293	United States
295.A-Z	Other regions or countries, A-Z
	Naval hospital corps
310	General works
	By region or country
320	United States

	Medical service
	Naval hospital corps
	By region or country -- Continued
325.A-Z	Other regions or countries, A-Z
	Nurse corps
	For biography see VG226+
350	General works
	By region or country
353	United States
355.A-Z	Other regions or countries, A-Z
	Naval hospital service and hospitals
	For hospitals and hospital service in a particular war, see the
	war in classes D-F
410	General works
	By region or country
	United States
	Cf. RA11.B15+ Public Health Service
	Cf. RA981.A4 Public Health Service hospitals
420	General works
424.A-Z	By region or state, A-Z
425.A-Z	By city, A-Z
430.A-Z	Other regions or countries, A-Z
450	Hospital ships
457	Red Cross at sea
	Medical and surgical handbooks, manuals, etc.
460	General works
	By region or country
463	United States
465.A-Z	Other regions or countries, A-Z
466	Sailors' first-aid manuals
	Naval hygiene. Sanitation and health
	Cf. UH600+ Military hygiene and sanitation
	Cf. V386 Protection and decontamination in atomic,
	biological, and chemical warfare
470	General works
471	General special
	Including diet, drinking water, liquor problems, tropical
	hygiene, venereal disease
	By region or country
473	United States
475.A-Z	Other regions or countries, A-Z
(478)	Rehabilitation of disabled sailors
	see UB360+
	Public relations. Press. War correspondents
	Cf. UH700+ Military public relations, press, etc.
500	General works
	By region or country

	Public relations. Press. War correspondents
	By region or country -- Continued
503	United States
505.A-Z	Other regions or countries, A-Z
	Civil engineering
590	General works
	By region or country
593	United States
	For Construction Battalion histories, etc. see VA66.C6+
595.A-Z	Other regions or countries, A-Z
	Artificers
	Including carpenters' mates, blacksmiths, painters, etc.
600	General works
	By region or country
603	United States
605.A-Z	Other regions or countries, A-Z
	Aerographers. Aerographers' mates
610	General works
	By region or country
613	United States
615.A-Z	Other regions or countries, A-Z
	Lithographers
635	General works
	By region or country
638	United States
639.A-Z	Other regions or countries, A-Z
	Electricians see VM471+
	Machinists. Machinists' mates
800	General works
	By region or country
803	United States
805.A-Z	Other regions or countries, A-Z
	Operations specialists. CIC personnel
820	General works
	By region or country
823	United States
825.A-Z	Other regions or countries, A-Z
	Utilitiesmen
880	General works
	By region or country
883	United States
885.A-Z	Other regions or countries, A-Z
	Yeomen. Clerical service
900	General works
	By region or country
903	United States
905.A-Z	Other regions or countries, A-Z

VG

	Engineering aides. Surveyors. Draftsmen
920	General works
	By region or country
923	United States
925.A-Z	Other regions or countries, A-Z
	Boatswains. Boatswains' mates
950	General works
	By region or country
953	United States
955.A-Z	Other regions or countries, A-Z
	Photographers. Photographers' mates
1010	General works
	By region or country
1013	United States
1015.A-Z	Other regions or countries, A-Z
1020	Photographic interpretation
	Instrumentmen
1030	General works
	By region or country
1033	United States
1035.A-Z	Other regions or countries, A-Z
	Social work. Social welfare services
2000	General works
	By region or country
2003	United States
2005.A-Z	Other regions or countries, A-Z
	Recreation and information services
2020	General works
	By region or country
	United States
2025	General works
2026	United States. Bureau of Naval Personnel. Special Services Division
2029.A-Z	Other regions or countries, A-Z

Navigation. Merchant marine
    Class here works on the technical aspects of navigation
    For the economic aspects of water transportation, including
        policy, shipping, institutions, carriers, etc. see HE380.8+
    Periodicals and societies. By language of publication

1	English
2	French
3	German
4	Other languages (not A-Z)
5	Congresses
	Museums. Exhibitions
6.A1	General works
6.A2-Z	By region or country, A-Z

      Under each country:

.x	*General works*
.x2A-.x2Z	*Special. By city, A-Z*

Abridgements of the nautical almanac, etc.
    Cf. QB8.A+ Nautical and air (aeronautical) almanacs

7	American
8	Other (not A-Z)
	Collected works (nonserial)
9	Several authors
11	Individual authors
	Dictionaries see V23+
	History, conditions, etc.
15	General works
	By period
16	Ancient
17	Medieval
	Including Viking ships
	Modern
18	General works
19	19th century
20	20th century
	By region or country
21	America
	North America
22	General works
	United States
23	General works
23.5	Confederate States
23.7	Great Lakes
24.A-.W	By state, A-W
25.A-Z	By city, A-Z
	Canada
26	General
27.A-Z	Subdivisions, A-Z

History, conditions, etc.
  By region or country
    Europe
      Great Britain -- Continued
64.A-Z   Cities (or other special), A-Z
      Austria
65   General
66.A-Z   Subdivisions, A-Z
      Belgium
67   General
68.A-Z   Subdivisions, A-Z
      Denmark
69   General
70.A-Z   Subdivisions, A-Z
      France
71   General
72.A-Z   Subdivisions, A-Z
      Germany
                   Including West Germany
73   General
74.A-Z   Subdivisions, A-Z
74.5   East Germany
      Greece
75   General
76.A-Z   Subdivisions, A-Z
76.5   Ireland (Éire)
      Netherlands
77   General
78.A-Z   Subdivisions, A-Z
      Italy
79   General
80.A-Z   Subdivisions, A-Z
      Norway
81   General
82.A-Z   Subdivisions, A-Z
      Portugal
83   General
84.A-Z   Subdivisions, A-Z
      Russia in Europe
85   General
86.A-Z   Subdivisions, A-Z
86.5   Scandinavia (General)
      Spain
87   General
88.A-Z   Subdivisions, A-Z
      Sweden
89   General

VK

Harbors. Ports
   Cf. HE550+ Economic aspects
   Cf. HE951+ Port guides, charges, etc.
   Cf. TC203+ Coast protective works, harbor engineering,
      etc.

321	General works
	By country see HE550+
345	Wharf management. Storage, etc.
358	Marine terminals
	Dock facilities
	Including bunkering, coaling, docking and repairing
361	General works
365.A-Z	By port, A-Z
367	Fuel stations

Marinas. Anchorages for small boats and yachts. Small
  craft refuge harbors
   Cf. TC352+ Hydraulic engineering

369	General works
	By region or country
	United States
369.5	General works
369.6.A-Z	By place, A-Z
369.8.A-Z	Other regions or countries, A-Z

   Under each country:
    .x   *General works*
    .x2A-.x2Z   *By place, A-Z*

Collisions and their prevention
  Including regulations, rules of the road, etc.
  Cf. VK1250+ Shipwrecks

371	General works
372	Rule of port helm
373	Lights and signals
(375-376)	Law
	see class K
	Cases. Investigations
(377)	General works
(378.A-Z)	Individual. By name of vessel, A-Z
(378.L3)	Larchmont (Steamer)

Signaling
  Cf. VK1000+ Lighthouse service
  Cf. V280+ Naval signaling

381	General works
382	Tests of sight and hearing
383	Fog signals
385	Flags
	Cf. V300+ Naval and marine flags
387	Lights

	Signaling -- Continued
388	Sound. Submarine signaling
389.A-Z	Special systems. By name of inventor, A-Z
391	Codes
	For national lists of ships with distinctive signal letters see HE565.A3+
391.I6A-.I6Z	International code of signals. By country, A-Z
	Further subarranged by date
	e.g.
391.I6U6 1956	United States, 1956
393	Funnel marks. House flags of navigation companies, etc.
397	Wireless telegraphy and telephony. Radio, radar, etc.
	Cf. VG76+ Naval wireless telegraphy, telephony, etc.
	Cf. VK560+ Electronics in navigation
	Cf. VM480+ Shipborne electronic equipment and installations
	Study and teaching
401	General works
405	Examinations, questions, etc.
	By region or country
421	America
	North America
422	General works
	United States
423	General works
423.5	Confederate States
423.7	Great Lakes
424.A-.W	By state, A-W
425.A-Z	By city, A-Z
	Canada
426	General
427.A-Z	Subdivisions, A-Z
427.5	Latin America (General)
	Mexico
428	General
429.A-Z	Subdivisions, A-Z
	Central America
430	General
431.A-Z	By region or country, A-Z
	West Indies
432	General
433.A-Z	By island or group of islands, A-Z
	South America
434	General works
	Argentina
436	General
437.A-Z	Subdivisions, A-Z

VK

Study and teaching
  By region or country
    South America -- Continued
      Bolivia

438	General
439.A-Z	Subdivisions, A-Z

      Brazil

441	General
442.A-Z	Subdivisions, A-Z

      Chile

443	General
444.A-Z	Subdivisions, A-Z

      Colombia

445	General
446.A-Z	Subdivisions, A-Z

      Ecuador

447	General
448.A-Z	Subdivisions, A-Z
449	Guyana
449.5	Suriname
450	French Guiana
451	Paraguay
452	Peru
453	Uruguay
454	Venezuela

    Europe

455	General works

      Great Britain

457	General works
459	England and Wales
461	Scotland
463	Northern Ireland
464.A-Z	Cities (or other special), A-Z

      Austria

465	General
466.A-Z	Subdivisions, A-Z

      Belgium

467	General
468.A-Z	Subdivisions, A-Z

      Denmark

469	General
470.A-Z	Subdivisions, A-Z

      France

471	General
472.A-Z	Subdivisions, A-Z

      Germany
        Including West Germany

Study and teaching
By region or country
Europe
Germany -- Continued
473 General
474.A-Z Subdivisions, A-Z
474.5 East Germany
Greece
475 General
476.A-Z Subdivisions, A-Z
476.5 Ireland (Éire)
Netherlands
477 General
478.A-Z Subdivisions, A-Z
Italy
479 General
480.A-Z Subdivisions, A-Z
Norway
481 General
482.A-Z Subdivisions, A-Z
Portugal
483 General
484.A-Z Subdivisions, A-Z
Russia in Europe
485 General
486.A-Z Subdivisions, A-Z
486.5 Scandinavia (General)
Spain
487 General
488.A-Z Subdivisions, A-Z
Sweden
489 General
490.A-Z Subdivisions, A-Z
Switzerland
491 General
492.A-Z Subdivisions, A-Z
Turkey see VK511+
496.A-Z Other European countries, A-Z
Asia
499 General works
China
501 General
502.A-Z Subdivisions, A-Z
India
503 General
504.A-Z Subdivisions, A-Z
Japan

VK

	Study and teaching
	By region or country
	Asia
	Japan -- Continued
505	General
506.A-Z	Subdivisions, A-Z
	Iran
507	General
508.A-Z	Subdivisions, A-Z
	Russia in Asia. Siberia
509	General
510.A-Z	Subdivisions, A-Z
	Turkey
511	General
512.A-Z	Subdivisions, A-Z
513.A-Z	Other Asian countries, A-Z
	Africa
515	General works
	Egypt
517	General
518.A-Z	Subdivisions, A-Z
519.A-Z	Other African countries, A-Z
	Australia
521	General
522.A-Z	Subdivisions, A-Z
522.5	New Zealand
	Pacific islands
523	General works
524.A-Z	By island or group of islands, A-Z
	Individual schools
525.A-Z	United States. By name of school, A-Z
529.A-Z	Other countries. By country and name of school, A-Z
	Training
531	General works
532	Training ships
533	Apprentices
	Officers
535	General works
537	Examinations
	Seamanship
541	General works
	Sailing. Helmsmanship
543	General works
	Small boat sailing see GV811.6
544	Sea scouting. Boy scouts. Girl scouts
545	Miscellaneous topics (not A-Z)
547	Devices for calming the waves. Use of oil in storms

Science of navigation
Including nautical astronomy
Cf. QB1+ Astronomy
Cf. SH343.8 Fisheries navigation
549   History
General works
551   Through 1700
553   1701-1800
555   1801-
559   General special
Including the nautical mile
559.3   Juvenile works
559.5   Examinations, questions, etc.
Electronics in navigation
Cf. VG76+ Naval wireless telegraph and telephone, radio, radar, etc.
Cf. VK397 Marine signaling
Cf. VM325 Electric and electronic equipment on small craft
Cf. VM480+ Shipborne electronic equipment and installation
560   General works
Loran tables
561.A1   General works
561.A2-Z   By region
561.A6   Asia (Coasts)
561.A7   Atlantic Ocean
561.P3   Pacific Ocean
United States (Coasts)
561.U5   General works
561.U57   West coast
562   Artificial satellites in ship navigation
563   Nautical tables
Including azimuth tables
Cf. QB8.A+ Nautical and air (aeronautical) almanacs
565   Latitude and longitude
Including tables
567   Longitude and time at sea
Including tables
569   Sumner's method. Sumner line
570   Optimum ship routing. Least time
571   Great circle sailing (Shortest distance)
571.5   Inertial navigation
572   Dead reckoning
Nautical instruments
Cf. GC41 Oceanographic instruments (General)
Cf. QB84.5+ Astronomical instruments

VK

	Nautical instruments -- Continued
573	General works
	Special instruments
(575)	Chronometers (Use on board ship)
	see QB107
577	Compass. Gyro compass
	Including use for sea, air, or land
	Cf. QC849 Magnetism of ships and deviation of compass
579	Distance finders, tables, calculations, etc.
581	Logs
	Cf. VK211 Logbooks
583	Sextant, quadrant, etc.
583.5	Inertial navigation systems
584.A-Z	Other instruments, A-Z
584.A7	Artificial horizon
584.A9	Automatic pilot
584.G8	Gyroscopic instruments
584.L37	Lasers
584.M34	Maneuvering boards
584.S55	Slide rule
584.S6	Sounding apparatus
	Cf. GC78.A+ Oceanographic instruments
584.S65	Spheroscope
584.S7	Station pointer
585	Catalogs
587	Other special topics (not A-Z)
	Including use of charts
	Cf. VK547 Devices for calming the waves
	Marine hydrography. Hydrographic surveying
	Cf. GA1+ Cartography
	Cf. GC1+ Oceanography
	Cf. QB301+ Geodetic surveying
	Cf. TA623 Hydrographic surveying for engineering purposes
	Cf. V396+ Military oceanography
588	Periodicals. Societies
	For individual countries see VK597.A+
	Cf. VK798 Sailing directions
589	Congresses
591	General works
593	General special
593.5	Methods of observation. Instruction for observers
594	Apparatus. Instruments (Collective and individual (not A-Z)
	Cf. VM453 Oceanographic research ships
595.A-Z	Individual voyages, A-Z

VK

Tide and current tables
By region or country
Atlantic Ocean -- Continued

625	North Sea (Dutch coast)
626	North Sea (Belgian coast)
	British Isles
627	General works
	West coast
628	General works
	Ireland see VK631
629	England (West Coast). St. George's Channel
630	Bristol Channel
631	Ireland. Irish Sea
632	Isle of Man
633	Scotland (West Coast)
634	Hebrides
635	Scotland (North and east coasts)
636	Shetland Islands
637	Orkney Islands
	England (East coast)
638	General works
638.5	Thames River
	English Channel
639	General works
641	British coast
	Channel Islands
643	General works
644.A-Z	By island, A-Z
	French coasts (General and English Channel)
645	General works
647	France (West coast). Bay of Biscay
	Spanish and Portuguese coasts (General and Atlantic)
649	General works
650.A-Z	Local, A-Z
	e.g.
650.C2	Cadiz, Gulf of
650.S3	Santander
651	Strait of Gibraltar
	Mediterranean Sea
653	General works
654	Spain
655	Balearic Islands
656	France. Gulf of Lyons
657	Italy
658	Gulf of Genoa. Ligurian Sea
659	Corsica
660	Sardinia

Tide and current tables
By region or country
Atlantic Ocean
Mediterranean Sea -- Continued

661	Tyrrhenian Sea
662	Sicily. Strait of Messina. Sicily Channel
	Including Skerki Bank
	Adriatic Sea and islands
663	General works
664	Yugoslav coast and islands
665	Turkey
666	Greece
667	Ionian Sea and islands
667.5	Crete
668	Aegean Sea and islands
669	Dardanelles. Sea of Marmora
670	Black Sea
671	Sea of Azov
	Eastern coasts
672	Asia Minor
673	Cyprus
674	Africa (North coast)
	African coast (General and West)
677	General works
	Atlantic islands
679	General works
680.A-Z	By island or group of islands, A-Z
680.A9	Azores
680.C2	Canary Islands
680.C3	Cape Verde Islands
680.M2	Madeira Islands
680.S2	Salvages
	Indian Ocean
685	General works
687	Africa (East coast)
687.1	South Africa
687.3	Mozambique
687.5	Tanzania
687.7	Kenya
687.8	Ethiopia. Somalia
689	Rivers
691	Islands
693	Gulf of Aden
695	Red Sea
697	Persian Gulf
698	Indian coast. Asia (South coast)
699	Arabian Sea

Tide and current tables
By region or country
Indian Ocean -- Continued
701 Bay of Bengal
Coasts of Asia (General and East)
702 General works
703 Gulf of Siam
705 China Sea and Chinese coast
706 Yangtze River and tributaries
707 Yellow Sea
709 Japan Sea. Japanese islands
710 Malaysia. Singapore
711 Philippines
Pacific Ocean. Pacific islands
715 General works
717 North Pacific
725 South Pacific
Special
727 Australia
729 New Zealand
731 Indonesia
733.A-Z Other islands or groups of islands, A-Z
Eastern Pacific. America (West coast)
741 General works
743 Alaska. Bering Sea and Strait
745 Canada (West coast).   British Columbia
746 Vancouver Island
United States (West coast)
747 General works
748.A-.W By state, A-W
749 Mexico (West coast)
Central America (West coast)
751 General works
752.A-Z Local, A-Z
South America (West coast)
755 General works
756.A-Z Local, A-Z
757 South Atlantic and South Pacific Oceans
Including West Indies, South America, and Pacific
Atlantic Ocean (General) see VK610
Atlantic Ocean (West)
759 General works
North America and coasts of Europe and Africa see
VK610+
South American coasts (General and East)
761 General works
763 Strait of Magellan

Tide and current tables
  By region or country
    Atlantic Ocean (West)
      South American coasts (General and East) -- Continued

764	Falkland Islands
765	Argentina
766	La Plata River
767	Brazil
768.A-Z	Other East South-American coasts, A-Z
	e.g.
768.G8	Guyana

      Central American and Mexican coasts (General and East)

| 769 | General works |
| 770.A-Z | Central America. Local, A-Z |

      West Indies. Caribbean Sea and Gulf of Mexico

| 771 | General works |
| 773.A-Z | By island or group of islands, A-Z |

      Gulf of Mexico

| 775 | General works |
| 777 | Florida Keys. Florida Strait. Windward Passage |

      United States (East coast)

781	General works
782.A-Z	Local, A-Z
	e.g.
782.C5	Chesapeake Bay

      Great Lakes

| 783 | General works |
| 784.A-Z | Individual lakes, etc., A-Z |

      Canada (East coast)

785	General works
786	Nova Scotia. Cape Breton Island
787	Bay of Fundy
788	Saint Lawrence River
789	Newfoundland and Labrador
790	Hudson Bay, Hudson Strait, etc.
791	Greenland
792	Baffin Bay, Davis Strait, etc.
793	United States as a whole
	Including island possessions
794	Canada as a whole

Sailing directions. Pilot guides

798	Serial publications
	Including hydrographic notices, notices to mariners, etc.
799	Tables for navigators. Distances etc.
	For nautical astronomy tables, see VK563+
800	History

Sailing directions. Pilot guides -- Continued
General works
801 Through 1800
802 1801-
(803) Official sailing directions published by Great Britain
see VK804+
By region or country
804 American waters as a whole
805 Antarctic regions
Arctic Ocean
807 General works
808 Canadian Arctic
Including archipelago passages
For Hudson Bay see VK990
For Baffin Bay see VK992
809 White Sea
Atlantic Ocean
For South Atlantic and American coasts, see VK957+
810 General works
North Atlantic
811 General works
813 General special. Steam lanes
North Atlantic islands
814.A1 General works
814.A3-Z By island or group of islands, A-Z
Azores see VK880.A9
814.F2 Faeroe Islands
814.I2 Iceland
Madeira Islands see VK880.M2
Orkney Islands see VK837
Shetland Islands see VK836
814.5 Scandinavia
North Sea
815 General works
816 Norway
817 Skagerrak
818 Kattegat. The Sound. The Belts
Baltic Sea
819 General works
820 Sweden
821 Soviet Union
821.5 Finland
821.8.A-Z Other, A-Z
e.g.
821.8.B6 Bothnia, Gulf of
822 German coasts (General and Baltic)
823 Danish coasts

Sailing directions. Pilot guides
By region or country
Atlantic Ocean -- Continued

824	North Sea (German coast)
825	North Sea (Dutch coast)
826	North Sea (Belgian coast)
	British Isles
827	General works
827.5	Inland waters
	West coast
828	General works
	Ireland see VK831
829	England (West coast). St. George's Channel
830	Bristol Channel
831	Ireland. Irish Sea
832	Isle of Man
833	Scotland (West coast)
834	Hebrides
834.5	East coast
835	Scotland (North and east coasts)
836	Shetland Islands
837	Orkney Islands
	England (East coast)
838	General works
838.5	Thames River
	English Channel
839	General works
841	British coast
	Channel Islands
843	General works
844.A-Z	Individual, A-Z
	French coasts (General and English Channel)
845	General works
847	France (West Coast). Bay of Biscay
	Spanish and Portuguese coasts (General and Atlantic)
849	General works
850.A-Z	Local, A-Z
	e.g.
850.C2	Cadiz, Gulf of
851	Strait of Gibraltar
	Mediterranean Sea
853	General works
854	Spain
855	Balearic Islands
856	France. Gulf of Lyons
857	Italy
858	Gulf of Genoa. Ligurian Sea

Sailing directions. Pilot guides
  By region or country
    Indian Ocean -- Continued

893	Gulf of Aden
895	Red Sea
897	Persian Gulf
898	Indian coast. Asia (South coast)
899	Arabian Sea
901	Bay of Bengal
	Coasts of Asia (General and East)
902	General works
903	Gulf of Siam
905	China Sea and Chinese coast
906	Yangtze River
907	Yellow Sea
909	Japan Sea. Japanese islands
910	Northeast coast of Asia
	Including Korea, Siberia and Sea of Okhotsk
911	Philippines
	Inland waters of Asia
913	Caspian Sea
914.A-Z	Other, A-Z
	e.g.
914.B3	Baikal, Lake
	Pacific Ocean. Pacific islands
915	General works
917	North Pacific
925	South Pacific
	Special
927	Australia
929	New Zealand
931	Indonesia. East Indies pilot (United States)
933.A-Z	Other islands or groups of islands, A-Z
	e.g.
933.H3	Hawaii
	Eastern Pacific. America (West coast)
941	General works
943	Alaska. Bering Sea and Strait
945	Canada (West coast). British Columbia
946	Vancouver Island
	United States (West coast)
947	General works
948.A-.W	By state, A-W
	Alaska see VK943
	Hawaii see VK933.H3
949	Mexico (West coast)
	Central America (West coast)

	Sailing directions. Pilot guides
	By region or country
	Pacific Ocean. Pacific islands
	Eastern Pacific. America (West coast)
	Central America (West coast) -- Continued
951	General works
952.A-Z	Local, A-Z
	South America (West coast)
955	General works
956.A-Z	Local, A-Z
957	South Atlantic and South Pacific Oceans
	Including West Indies, South America, and Pacific
	Atlantic Ocean (General) see VK810
	Atlantic Ocean (West)
959	General works
	South American coasts (General and East)
	South American coasts (General and East)
961	General works
962	Tierra del Fuego
963	Strait of Magellan
964	Falkland Islands
965	Argentina
	Cf. VK962 Tierra del Fuego
966	La Plata River
967	Brazil
967.5	Amazon River
968.A-Z	Other East South-American coasts, A-Z
	e.g.
968.F8	French Guiana
	Central American and Mexican coasts (General and East)
969	General works
970.A-Z	Central America. Local, A-Z
970.P2	Panama Canal
	West Indies. Caribbean Sea. Gulf of Mexico
971	General works
973.A-Z	By island or group of islands, A-Z
	e.g.
973.P7	Puerto Rico
	Gulf of Mexico
975	General works
977	Florida Keys. Florida Strait. Windward Passage
	United States (East coast). "Atlantic coast pilots"
	Including "inland waterway," "inside route"
	For sectional guides see VK982.A+
981	General works

	Sailing directions. Pilot guides
	By region or country
	Atlantic Ocean (West)
	United States (East coast). "Atlantic coast pilots" --
	Continued
982.A-Z	Local, A-Z
	e.g.
982.C5	Chesapeake Bay
982.N5	New Jersey coast
	Great Lakes
983	General works
984.A-Z	Individual lakes, etc., A-Z
	e.g.
984.G4	Georgian Bay
984.O6	Lake Ontario
	Canada (East coast)
985	General works
	Inland waters
985.4	General works
985.5.A-Z	Special, A-Z
985.5.O88	Ottawa River (Quebec and Ontario)
986	Nova Scotia. Cape Breton Island
987	Bay of Fundy
987.7	Saint John River
988	Saint Lawrence River
989	Newfoundland and Labrador
990	Hudson Bay, Hudson Strait, etc.
991	Greenland
992	Baffin Bay, Davis Strait, etc.
	Canada (Arctic coast) see VK808
	United States as a whole
	Including island possessions (General); depth of channels
	and harbors
993	General works
	Alaska see VK943
	Hawaii see VK933.H3
	Puerto Rico see VK973.P7
	East coast see VK981+
	West coast see VK947+
	Inland waters
	For "inland waterway," "inside route" (Atlantic coast)
	see VK981+
994	General works
995.A-Z	Special, A-Z
	e.g.
	Great Lakes see VK983+
995.O4	Ohio River

	Sailing directions. Pilot guides
	By region or country -- Continued
	Inland waters
	Asia see VK913+
	Europe
996	General works
997.A-Z	Special, A-Z
	e.g.
	British Isles see VK827.5
997.R5	Rhine River
	Thames River see VK838.5
	Lighthouse service
	Including lighthouses, lightships, beacons, buoys and buoyage, foghorns, etc.
1000	Periodicals. Societies
1005	Congresses
1010	General works
1012	Buoys and buoyage (General)
1013	General special
1015	History
	By region or country
1021	America
	North America
1022	General works
	United States
	Bureau of Lighthouses (to 1959). Coast Guard jurisdiction, 1939-
1023.A2	Annual reports
1023.A21-.A24	Other serials
1023.A25	Special reports. By date
1023.A3	Orders
1023.A4	Collections
1023.A5	Instructions
	Laws and regulations see KF2588.5
1023.A7	Miscellaneous. By date
	General United States
1023.A8	Other official bodies
1023.A9-.Z8	Nonofficial publications
1023.Z9	Miscellaneous uncataloged material
1023.3	Great Lakes
1024.A-Z	By region or state, A-Z
1025.A-Z	Special lighthouses, A-Z
	e.g.
1025.D5	Diamond Shoals
1025.M5	Minot's Ledge
	Canada
1026	General

	Lighthouse service
	By region or country
	North America
	Canada -- Continued
1027.A-Z	Subdivisions, A-Z
1027.5	Latin America (General)
	Mexico
1028	General
1029.A-Z	Subdivisions, A-Z
	Central America
1030	General
1031.A-Z	By region or country, A-Z
	West Indies
1032	General
1033.A-Z	By island or group of islands, A-Z
	South America
1034	General works
	Argentina
1036	General
1037.A-Z	Subdivisions, A-Z
	Bolivia
1038	General
1039.A-Z	Subdivisions, A-Z
	Brazil
1041	General
1042.A-Z	Subdivisions, A-Z
	Chile
1043	General
1044.A-Z	Subdivisions, A-Z
	Colombia
1045	General
1046.A-Z	Subdivisions, A-Z
	Ecuador
1047	General
1048.A-Z	Subdivisions, A-Z
1049	Guyana
1049.5	Suriname
1050	French Guiana
1051	Paraguay
1052	Peru
1053	Uruguay
1054	Venezuela
	Europe
1055	General works
	Great Britain
1057	General works
1059	England and Wales

Lighthouse service
By region or country
Europe
Great Britain -- Continued
1061	Scotland
1063	Northern Ireland
1064.A-Z	Cities (or other special), A-Z
	Austria
1065	General
1066.A-Z	Subdivisions, A-Z
	Belgium
1067	General
1068.A-Z	Subdivisions, A-Z
	Denmark
1069	General
1070.A-Z	Subdivisions, A-Z
	France
1071	General
1072.A-Z	Subdivisions, A-Z
	Germany
	Including West Germany
1073	General
1074.A-Z	Subdivisions, A-Z
1074.5	East Germany
	Greece
1075	General
1076.A-Z	Subdivisions, A-Z
1076.5	Ireland (Éire)
	Netherlands
1077	General
1078.A-Z	Subdivisions, A-Z
	Italy
1079	General
1080.A-Z	Subdivisions, A-Z
	Norway
1081	General
1082.A-Z	Subdivisions, A-Z
	Portugal
1083	General
1084.A-Z	Subdivisions, A-Z
	Russia in Europe
1085	General
1086.A-Z	Subdivisions, A-Z
1086.5	Scandinavia (General)
	Spain
1087	General
1088.A-Z	Subdivisions, A-Z

	Lighthouse service
	By region or country
	Europe -- Continued
	Sweden
1089	General
1090.A-Z	Subdivisions, A-Z
	Switzerland
1091	General
1092.A-Z	Subdivisions, A-Z
	Turkey see VK1111+
1096.A-Z	Other European countries, A-Z
	Asia
1099	General works
	China
1101	General
1102.A-Z	Subdivisions, A-Z
	India
1103	General
1104.A-Z	Subdivisions, A-Z
	Japan
1105	General
1106.A-Z	Subdivisions, A-Z
	Iran
1107	General
1108.A-Z	Subdivisions, A-Z
	Russia in Asia. Siberia
1109	General
1110.A-Z	Subdivisions, A-Z
	Turkey
1111	General
1112.A-Z	Subdivisions, A-Z
	Africa
1115	General works
	Egypt
1117	General
1118.A-Z	Subdivisions, A-Z
1119.A-Z	Other African countries, A-Z
	Australia
1121	General
1122.A-Z	Subdivisions, A-Z
1122.5	New Zealand
	Pacific Islands
1123	General works
1124.A-Z	By island or group of islands, A-Z
	Biography
1139	Collective
1140.A-Z	Individual, A-Z

VK

	Lighthouse service -- Continued
	Lists of lights, buoys, beacons, etc.
	Including electronic beacons, e. g. Racons
1150	General lists
	By region or country
	Europe
1151	General works
	Great Britain
1153	General works
1155	England
1157	Scotland
1159	Ireland
1161	Norway
1163	Denmark
1165	Sweden
1167	Russia
1169	Germany
	Including West Germany
1170	East Germany
1171	Netherlands
1173	France
1175	Portugal
1176	Mediterranean Sea
1177	Spain
1179	Italy
1181	Greece
(1183)	Turkey
	see VK1209.T9
1185.A-Z	Other European regions or countries, A-Z
	e.g.
1185.B3	Barents Sea
1185.E7	Estonia
1185.F5	Finland, Gulf of
	Africa
1190	General works
1191	East Africa
	Cf. VK1209.R4 Red Sea
1192	West Africa
1193	Morocco
1194	Nigeria
1195	Somalia
1196	South Africa
1197.A-Z	Portuguese Africa, A-Z
1198	Egypt
1199.A-Z	Other African regions or countries, A-Z
	Asia
1203	China

Lighthouse service
    Lists of lights, buoys, beacons, etc.
        By region or country
            Asia -- Continued

1204	India
1205	Southeast Asia. Indochina
1206	Indonesia. Malaysia
1207	Japan
1208	Russia in Asia. Siberia
1209.A-Z	Other Asian regions or countries, A-Z
	e.g.
1209.R4	Red Sea
1209.T9	Turkey
1211	Australia
1212	New Zealand
1214	Pacific Ocean
	Pacific islands
1221	General works
1223.A-Z	By island or group of islands, A-Z
	South America
1225	General works
1226	Argentina
1227	Bolivia
1228	Brazil
1229	Chile
1230	Colombia
1231	Ecuador
1232	Guyana
1233	Paraguay
1234	Peru
1235	Uruguay
1236	Venezuela
	Central America
1237	General works
1238.A-Z	By region or country, A-Z
	West Indies
1239	General works
1240.A-Z	By island or group of islands, A-Z
	North America
1241	General works

VK

Lighthouse service
    Lists of lights, buoys, beacons, etc.
        By region or country
            North America -- Continued
                United States
                    On June 17, 1910, the United States Lighthouse Board was superseded by the United States Bureau of Lighthouses
                    The districts whose numbers were changed were 9th district (old) to 12th district (new); 12th district (old) to 13th district (new); 13th district (old) to 15th district (new); 15th district (old) to 16th district (new); 3d subdistrict (old) became 9th district (new); and 12th subdistrict (old) became 19th district (new). Old districts 1-8, 10, 11, and 14 remain unchanged as to number
                    Publications after June 17, 1910, are to be distinguished in that the new 9th, 12th, 13th, 15th, and 16th are to be marked 9tha, 12tha, 13tha, 15tha, and 16tha. Other districts need no distinguishing letter

1243	General works
1244	Great Lakes
1245	Canada
1246	Mexico

    Bridge lights

1247	General works

        By region or country

1248	United States
1249.A-Z	Other regions or countries, A-Z

Shipwrecks and fires
    Including reports and examinations
    For narratives see G521+

1250	General works
1255.A-Z	Ships wrecked, A-Z

    e.g.

1255.T6	Titanic (Steamship)
1255.V4	Vestris (Steamboat)
1257.A-Z	Ships lost by fire, A-Z

    e.g.

1257.L3	Lafayette (Steamship)

        Formerly the "Normandie"
        Cf. VM383.N6 Normandie (Steamship)

1257.L4	Lexington (Steamboat)
1257.M6	Morro Castle (Steamship)
1258	Fire prevention and extinction

    Including lightning conductors, fire boats, fire sprinklers, etc.

	Shipwrecks and fires -- Continued
1259	Miscellaneous topics (not A-Z)
	Including abandoning ship, food supply
1265	Submarine disasters
	Cf. VK1491 Salvage
	Cf. VM975+ Diving
	By region or country
	United States
1270	General works
1271	Great Lakes
1272.A-Z	Other regions, A-Z
1273.A-.W	By state, A-W
	Canada. British America
1274	General works
1275.A-Z	By region, A-Z
1276.A-Z	By province, island, etc., A-Z
1276.B3	Bahama Islands
	Latin America
1277	General works
1278.A-Z	By region, A-Z
1279.A-Z	By country, island, etc., A-Z
	Europe
1280	General works
1281.A-Z	By region, A-Z
1282.A-Z	By country, A-Z
	Africa
1283	General works
1284.A-Z	By region, A-Z
1285.A-Z	By country, A-Z
	Asia
1286	General works
1287.A-Z	By region, A-Z
1288.A-Z	By country, A-Z
	Australia
1289	General works
1290.A-Z	By region, A-Z
1291.A-Z	By state or territory, A-Z
	New Zealand
1291.2	General works
1291.3.A-Z	By region, A-Z
	Pacific islands
1292	General works
1293.A-Z	By region, A-Z
1294.A-Z	By island or group of islands, A-Z
1297	Derelicts and their removal

VK

Shipwrecks and fires -- Continued

1299	Icebergs and navigation
	Including international ice observations, ice patrol service, etc.
	Cf. GB2401+ Icebergs (Physical geography)
	Icebreaking operations
1299.5	General works
1299.6.A-Z	By place, A-Z
	e.g.
1299.6.A7	Arctic regions
1299.6.G7	Great Lakes
	Saving of life and property
	Lifesaving
1300	Periodicals. Societies
1301	Congresses
1315	History
	By region or country
1321	America
	North America
1322	General works
	United States
1323	General works
1323.5	Confederate States
1323.7	Great Lakes
1324.A-.W	By state, A-W
1325.A-Z	By city, A-Z
	Canada
1326	General
1327.A-Z	Subdivisions, A-Z
1327.5	Latin America (General)
	Mexico
1328	General
1329.A-Z	Subdivisions, A-Z
	Central America
1330	General
1331.A-Z	By region or country, A-Z
	West Indies
1332	General
1333.A-Z	By island or group of islands, A-Z
	South America
1334	General works
	Argentina
1336	General
1337.A-Z	Subdivisions, A-Z
	Bolivia
1338	General
1339.A-Z	Subdivisions, A-Z
	Brazil

Saving of life and property
   Lifesaving
      By region or country
         Europe
            Germany -- Continued

1374.5	East Germany
	Greece
1375	General
1376.A-Z	Subdivisions, A-Z
1376.5	Ireland (Éire)
	Netherlands
1377	General
1378.A-Z	Subdivisions, A-Z
	Italy
1379	General
1380.A-Z	Subdivisions, A-Z
	Norway
1381	General
1382.A-Z	Subdivisions, A-Z
	Portugal
1383	General
1384.A-Z	Subdivisions, A-Z
	Russia in Europe
1385	General
1386.A-Z	Subdivisions, A-Z
1386.5	Scandinavia (General)
	Spain
1387	General
1388.A-Z	Subdivisions, A-Z
	Sweden
1389	General
1390.A-Z	Subdivisions, A-Z
	Switzerland
1391	General
1392.A-Z	Subdivisions, A-Z
	Turkey see VK1411+
1396.A-Z	Other European countries, A-Z
	Asia
1399	General works
	China
1401	General
1402.A-Z	Subdivisions, A-Z
	India
1403	General
1404.A-Z	Subdivisions, A-Z
	Japan
1405	General

	Saving of life and property
	Lifesaving
	By region or country
	Asia
	Japan -- Continued
1406.A-Z	Subdivisions, A-Z
	Iran
1407	General
1408.A-Z	Subdivisions, A-Z
	Russia in Asia. Siberia
1409	General
1410.A-Z	Subdivisions, A-Z
	Turkey
1411	General
1412.A-Z	Subdivisions, A-Z
1413.A-Z	Other Asian countries, A-Z
	Africa
1415	General works
	Egypt
1417	General
1418.A-Z	Subdivisions, A-Z
1419.A-Z	Other African countries, A-Z
	Australia
1421	General
1422.A-Z	Subdivisions, A-Z
1422.5	New Zealand
	Pacific islands
1423	General works
1424.A-Z	By island or group of islands, A-Z
	Biography
1430.A1	Collective
1430.A2-Z	Individual, A-Z
1445	General works
1447	General special
	Apparatus, stations, etc.
	Cf. VK383 Fog signals
	General works
1460.A-Z	Documents. By country, A-Z
1461	Treatises, etc.
	Appliances and means of lifesaving on ships
1462.A-Z	Documents. By country, A-Z
1463	General works
1471	General special
1473	Boats. Lifeboats
1474	Submarine rescue vehicles
1475	Buoys
1477	Life preservers

Pilots and pilotage
By region or country
North America
West Indies -- Continued

1533.A-Z	By island or group of islands, A-Z
	South America
1534	General works
	Argentina
1536	General
1537.A-Z	Subdivisions, A-Z
	Bolivia
1538	General
1539.A-Z	Subdivisions, A-Z
	Brazil
1541	General
1542.A-Z	Subdivisions, A-Z
	Chile
1543	General
1544.A-Z	Subdivisions, A-Z
	Colombia
1545	General
1546.A-Z	Subdivisions, A-Z
	Ecuador
1547	General
1548.A-Z	Subdivisions, A-Z
1549	Guyana
1549.5	Suriname
1550	French Guiana
1551	Paraguay
1552	Peru
1553	Uruguay
1554	Venezuela
	Europe
1555	General works
	Great Britain
1557	General works
1559	England and Wales
1561	Scotland
1563	Northern Ireland
1564.A-Z	Cities (or other special), A-Z
	Austria
1565	General
1566.A-Z	Subdivisions, A-Z
	Belgium
1567	General
1568.A-Z	Subdivisions, A-Z
	Denmark

VK

Pilots and pilotage
  By region or country
    Asia -- Continued
      China

1601	General
1602.A-Z	Subdivisions, A-Z

      India

1603	General
1604.A-Z	Subdivisions, A-Z

      Japan

1605	General
1606.A-Z	Subdivisions, A-Z

      Iran

1607	General
1608.A-Z	Subdivisions, A-Z

      Russia in Asia. Siberia

1609	General
1610.A-Z	Subdivisions, A-Z

      Turkey

1611	General
1612.A-Z	Subdivisions, A-Z
1613.A-Z	Other Asian countries, A-Z

    Africa

1615	General works

      Egypt

1617	General
1618.A-Z	Subdivisions, A-Z
1619.A-Z	Other African countries, A-Z

    Australia

1621	General
1622.A-Z	Subdivisions, A-Z
1622.5	New Zealand

    Pacific islands

1623	General works
1624.A-Z	By island or group or islands, A-Z
1645	General works
1661	General special

	Naval architecture. Shipbuilding. Marine engineering
	For war vessels (Construction, armament, etc.) see V750+
	Periodicals and societies. By language of publication
1	English
2	French
3	German
4	Other languages (not A-Z)
5	Congresses
	Museums. Exhibitions
6.A1	General works
6.A2-Z	By region or country

Under each country:

.x	*General works*
.x2A-.x2Z	*Special. By city, A-Z*

7	Collected works (nonserial)
	Dictionaries and encyclopedias see V23+
12	Directories
	History
15	General works
16	Ancient
17	Medieval
	Including Viking ships, cogs, etc.
	Modern
18	General works
19	19th century
20	20th century
	By region or country
	For individual companies, shipyards, etc. see VM301.A+
21	America
	North America
22	General works
	United States
23	General works
23.5	Confederate States
23.7	Great Lakes
24.A-.W	By state, A-W
25.A-Z	By city, A-Z
	Canada
26	General
27.A-Z	Subdivisions, A-Z
27.5	Latin America (General)
	Mexico
28	General
29.A-Z	Subdivisions, A-Z
	Central America
30	General

VM

	Biography
	Individual -- Continued
140.M8	Morey, Samuel
140.R8	Rumsey, James
140.T3	Taylor, David Watson
	Naval architecture (General)
	Cf. VM156+ Principles of naval architecture
	Cf. VM751+ Resistance and propulsion of ships
	Wooden ships
	General works
142	Through 1800
143	1801-1860
144	1861-
145	General works, 1861-
	Metal ships
146	Steel and iron ships
146.3	Aluminum ship structures
147	Miscellaneous topics (not A-Z)
	Including riveting and welding
	For underwater welding see VM965
148	Concrete ships
	Cf. VM323 Concrete boats
148.5	Plastic ships
149	Miscellaneous topics (not A-Z)
	Including dry rot, economy in shipbuilding, launching of ships
150	Juvenile works
151	Tables, pocketbooks, handbooks of ship calculations, etc.
	Special types of ships see VM311+
153	Tonnage tables (Tonnage of ships)
	Cf. HE737+ Tables and calculations for freight measurements
155	Measurement of ships
	Theory of the ship. Principles of naval architecture
156	General works
157	Displacement and buoyance of ships
159	Statistical stability of ships
161	Oscillations of ships
	Including rolling, etc.
162	Strength of materials in ships
163	Stresses and strains experienced by ships
	Resistance of ships see VM751+
	Study and teaching
165	General works
168	Problems, exercises, etc.
	By region or country
171	America

VM

Study and teaching
  By region or country
    South America -- Continued

201	Paraguay
202	Peru
203	Uruguay
204	Venezuela
	Europe
205	General works
	Great Britain
207	General works
209	England and Wales
211	Scotland
213	Northern Ireland
214.A-Z	Cities (or other special), A-Z
	Austria
215	General
216.A-Z	Subdivisions, A-Z
	Belgium
217	General
218.A-Z	Subdivisions, A-Z
	Denmark
219	General
220.A-Z	Subdivisions, A-Z
	France
221	General
222.A-Z	Subdivisions, A-Z
	Germany
	Including West Germany
223	General
224.A-Z	Subdivisions, A-Z
224.5	East Germany
	Greece
225	General
226.A-Z	Subdivisions, A-Z
226.5	Ireland (Éire)
	Netherlands
227	General
228.A-Z	Subdivisions, A-Z
	Italy
229	General
230.A-Z	Subdivisions, A-Z
	Norway
231	General
232.A-Z	Subdivisions, A-Z
	Portugal

VM

	Study and teaching
	By region or country
	Africa
	Egypt -- Continued
268.A-Z	Subdivisions, A-Z
269.A-Z	Other African countries, A-Z
	Australia
271	General
272.A-Z	Subdivisions, A-Z
272.5	New Zealand
	Pacific islands
273	General works
274.A-Z	By island or group or islands, A-Z
	Special schools
275.A-Z	United States. By place, A-Z
276.A-Z	Other countries. By country and by place, A-Z
285	Addresses, essays, lectures
287	Standards
291	Estimates
293	Marine standards
	Contracts and specifications
	Cf. VM737 Specifications for marine engines and boilers
295	General works
296.A-Z	Special, A-Z
	United States government vessels
296.U3	General works
296.U4	Coast and Geodetic Survey
296.U5	Coast Guard
	Bureau of Lighthouses
296.U6A-.U6Z	By name of vessel, A-Z
	e.g.
296.U6A5	Albatross (Screw steamer)
296.U6A8	Aster (Lighthouse tender)
296.U6S8	Sumac (Lighthouse tender)
296.U7	By number of vessel
	e.g.
296.U7 no.74	Lighthouse vessel, no. 74
296.U75	Quartermaster Corps
296.U8	Shipping Board
297	Designs and drawings
	Including blueprints and blueprint reading
297.5	Laying out. Lofting
	Ship models. Steamboat models
	Cf. VM6.A1+ Naval museums
	Cf. VM332 Yacht models
	Cf. VM342 Motorboat models

	Ship models. Steamboat models -- Continued
298	General works
298.3	Ship models in bottles
	Shipbuilding industry. Shipyards
298.5	General works
299	Management of works
299.5	Finance
	Including government aid, loans, and mortgage insurance
	By region or country
299.6	United States
	Cf. HE745+ Merchant marine (General)
299.7.A-Z	Other regions or countries, A-Z
300	Shop rates, costs, etc.
	Cf. HF5686.S5 Accounting
301.A-Z	Shipbuilding companies and shipyards, A-Z
	Including reports, catalogs, illustrations, history, etc.
307	Illustrations of ships of all kinds. Pictorial works
	Cf. N8230 Ships in art
	Cf. ND1370+ Marine painting
	Cf. NE957+ Naval prints
308	Ship decoration and ornament. Figureheads of ships
	Cf. VM382 Passenger ships
	Special types of vessels
	Cf. VM142+ Wooden ships
	Cf. VM146 Steel and iron ships
	Cf. VM148 Concrete ships
	Cf. VM295+ Specifications for vessels
	Cf. VM737 Specifications for marine engines
311.A-Z	By construction or rigging, A-Z
311.B3	Barges
311.B57	Birlings
311.B8	Bugeyes
311.C24	Caïques
311.C27	Caravels
311.C3	Catamarans. Double-bottom or multiple-hulled vessels
311.C33	Catboats
	Double-bottom or multiple-hulled vessels see VM311.C3
311.F7	Fore and afters
311.G3	Gabares
311.G33	Gaff-rigged vessels
311.R32	Rabelos
311.S38	Saveiros
311.S53	Sharpies
311.S7	Square-rigged ships
311.T7	Trabacolos
311.W5	Whalebacks

	Special types of vessels -- Continued
	Motor ships
315.A1-.A49	Periodicals. Societies
315.A5-Z	General works
317	Atomic ships. Nuclear-powered ships
	Cf. V857.5 Atomic submarine
	Small craft
	Cf. SH452.9.B58 Sport fishing boats
320	Periodicals. Societies
321	General works
	Boatyards
321.5	General works
321.52.A-Z	By region or country, A-Z
322	Maintenance and repair
323	Concrete boats
325	Electric and electronic equipment
	Cf. VK560+ Electronics in navigation
	Cf. VM347 Electric motors
	Cf. VM471+ Electricity on ships
	Cf. VM480+ Electronics on ships
	Cf. VM493 Electric lighting of ships
	Yachts
	Cf. GV811.8+ Yachting
331	General works
332	Models
333	Catalogs
335	Houseboats
	Motorboats. Launches
	Including gasoline and other combustion motors
	Cf. GV833.5+ Motorboats and motorboating (General)
340	Periodicals. Societies
341	General works
342	Models
343	Steam motorboats
	Electric boats
345	General works
347	Electric motors
348	Outboard motorboats
348.5	Jet boats. Jet-propelled craft
349	Catalogs
	Boats. Rowboats, small sailboats, etc.
	Cf. GN440+ Primitive transportation
351	General works
	Special
352	Rafts
353	Canoes

Special types of vessels
Small craft
Boats. Rowboats, small sailboats, etc.
Special -- Continued
355   Skiffs
357   Odd craft: Folding boats, water bicycles, etc.
359   Toy boats. Models
360   Inflatable boats
361   Catalogs, price lists, etc.
362   Hydrofoil boats
363   Ground effect machines for use over bodies of water
Submarine boats
Cf. V210+ Submarine warfare
Cf. V858+ Submarine boats in special navies
365   General works
366   Models
367.A-Z   Fittings, equipment, etc., A-Z
367.F83   Fuel cells
367.H6   Hooks
367.P4   Periscopes
Plastic viewports see VM367.P56
367.P56   Plastic windows. Plastic viewports
367.S3   Safety appliances
367.S63   Snorkels
367.S7   Storage batteries
371   Miscellaneous types of vessels
Including Arab dhows, Chinese junks
By use
378   General works
(380)   Warships
see V750+
Passenger ships
381   General works
382   Furnishings and decoration
383.A-Z   Individual ships, A-Z
Including their history, construction, etc.
e.g.
383.A6   Aquitania
383.B7   Bremen
383.G7   Great Eastern
383.L3   Leviathan
383.M27   Mariefred
383.M3   Mauretania
383.N6   Normandie
Cf. VK1257.L3 Lafayette (Steamship)
383.O4   Olympic

VM

	Special types of vessels
	By use
	Passenger ships
	Individual ships, A-Z -- Continued
383.Q3	Queen Elizabeth
383.Q32	Queen Elizabeth 2
383.Q4	Queen Mary
385.A-Z	Individual steamship lines, A-Z
	Including descriptions of facilities and vessels, views of the line, etc.
	For American interior navigation companies see HE633.A+
	For American coastal shipping companies see HE753.A+
	For ocean steamship companies see HE945.A2+
385.F3	Fall River Line
	Cargo ships
	Cf. VM385.A+ Individual steamship lines
391	General works
393.A-Z	Special. By type, A-Z
393.B37	Barge-carrying ships
393.B7	Bulk carriers
393.C65	Container ships
393.I64	Indiamen
393.R64	Roll-on/roll-off ships
395.A-Z	Individual vessels, A-Z
	e.g.
395.B5	Bluenose (Schooner)
395.C8	Cutty Sark (Clipper ship)
395.K5	Kliyūbātrā (Steamship)
396	Inland waterway vessels
397	Coast guard vessels
401	Colliers
	Dredges see TC188
421	Ferryboats
	For railway ferries see TF320
425	Coastal vessels
431	Fishing boats
451	Icebreaking vessels
451.5	Ice-strengthened vessels
452	Research vessels
453	Oceanographic research ships
	Cf. GC41 Oceanographic instruments
	Cf. GC67 Oceanographic submersibles
	Cf. VK594 Marine hydrographic instruments
	Tank vessels. Oil tankers

	Special types of vessels
	By use
	Tank vessels. Oil tankers -- Continued
455	General works
455.3	Chemical carriers
456	Liquefied gas carriers
457	Ore carriers
459	Refrigerated ships
460	Lake vessels
	River steamers
461	General works
461.5.A-Z	Individual vessels, A-Z
	e.g.
461.5.C6	Coonawarra (Riverboat)
461.5.D4	Delta Queen (Steamboat)
461.5.J43	Jeanie Deans (Steamboat)
461.5.K73	Krabben
461.5.M3	Mary Powell (Ship)
461.5.Y84	Yukon (Steamer)
463	Scows, lighters, etc.
464	Towboats. Tugboats
465	Whaling ships
	Cf. SH381.7 Whaling
466.A-Z	Other, A-Z
466.B3	Barges
466.C3	Cable ships
466.L8	Lumber ships. Timber ships
466.O35	Offshore support vessels
466.P54	Pilot boats
466.R4	Repair ships
466.S4	Search and rescue boats
466.S67	Stone-carrying vessels
467	Ship joinery
	Structural arrangements of ships
468	General works
469	Watertight compartments. Bulkhead construction
469.5	Pontoons and pontoon gear
	Cf. TC357 Piers
	Cf. TC363 Floating docks
	Cf. VM931 Ship-raising pontoons
470	Ship fitting, equipment, etc.
	For marine engines, appliances, etc. see VM731+
	Cf. VM367.A+ Submarine boat fittings, equipment, etc.
470.5	Ship supplies. Chandlers
	Uses of electricity on ships
	Cf. VM325 Electric and electronic equipment on small craft

VM

	Water supply -- Continued
505	Distillation of sea water
	Cf. G149+ Instructions for travellers
	Cf. Q116 Handbooks for scientific expeditions
511	Berthing, hammocks, etc.
	Means of propulsion
	Cf. VM751+ Resistance and propulsion of ships
521	General works
	Special topics
	Rigging, masts, spars, sails, etc.
531	General works
532	Sails and sailmaking
533	Knots, splices, etc.
541	Paddle wheels
	Screw propellers see VM755
561	Oars, paddles, etc.
562	Flippers, fins, oscillating foils
565	Steerage of ships
	Cf. VK541+ Seamanship (General)
	Cf. VM841+ Steering gear
	Marine engineering
	Including steam navigation
595	Periodicals. Societies
597	Dictionaries and encyclopedias
600	General works
605	General special
607	Pocketbooks, tables, manuals, etc.
	History
615	General works
618	Fulton-Livingston monopoly
	Cf. VM140.F9 Robert Fulton
619	Rumsey-Fitch controversy
	Cf. VM140.F5 John Fitch
	Cf. VM140.R8 James Rumsey
	By region or country
621	America
	North America
622	General works
	United States
	General
	Bureau of Engineering
623.A1	General works
623.A2	Annual reports
623.A4	Nonserial documents. By date
623.A5	Nonofficial publications. By date
623.A81-.A89	Other official (except naval)

VM

Marine engineering
By region or country
North America
United States
General -- Continued

623.A9-Z	Other nonoffical
623.5	Confederate States
623.7	Great Lakes
624.A-.W	By state, A-W
625.A-Z	By city, A-Z
	Canada
626	General works
627.A-Z	Subdivisions, A-Z
627.5	Latin America (General)
	Mexico
628	General
629.A-Z	Subdivisions, A-Z
	Central America
630	General
631.A-Z	By region or country, A-Z
	West Indies
632	General
633.A-Z	By island or group of islands, A-Z
	South America
634	General works
	Argentina
636	General
637.A-Z	Subdivisions, A-Z
	Bolivia
638	General
639.A-Z	Subdivisions, A-Z
	Brazil
641	General
642.A-Z	Subdivisions, A-Z
	Chile
643	General
644.A-Z	Subdivisions, A-Z
	Colombia
645	General
646.A-Z	Subdivisions, A-Z
	Ecuador
647	General
648.A-Z	Subdivisions, A-Z
649	Guyana
649.5	Suriname
650	French Guiana

	Marine engineering
	By region or country
	South America -- Continued
651	Paraguay
652	Peru
653	Uruguay
654	Venezuela
	Europe
655	General works
	Great Britain
657	General works
659	England and Wales
661	Scotland
663	Northern Ireland
664.A-Z	Cities (or other special), A-Z
	Austria
665	General
666.A-Z	Subdivisions, A-Z
	Belgium
667	General
668.A-Z	Subdivisions, A-Z
	Denmark
669	General
670.A-Z	Subdivisions, A-Z
	France
671	General
672.A-Z	Subdivisions, A-Z
	Germany
	Including West Germany
673	General
674.A-Z	Subdivisions, A-Z
674.5	East Germany
	Greece
675	General
676.A-Z	Subdivisions, A-Z
676.5	Ireland (Éire)
	Netherlands
677	General
678.A-Z	Subdivisions, A-Z
	Italy
679	General
680.A-Z	Subdivisions, A-Z
	Norway
681	General
682.A-Z	Subdivisions, A-Z
	Portugal

VM

Marine engineering
By region or country
Europe
Portugal -- Continued
683   General
684.A-Z   Subdivisions, A-Z
Russia in Europe
685   General
686.A-Z   Subdivisions, A-Z
686.5   Scandinavia (General)
Spain
687   General
688.A-Z   Subdivisions, A-Z
Sweden
689   General
690.A-Z   Subdivisions, A-Z
Switzerland
691   General
692.A-Z   Subdivisions, A-Z
Turkey see VM711+
696.A-Z   Other European countries, A-Z
Asia
699   General works
China
701   General
702.A-Z   Subdivisions, A-Z
India
703   General
704.A-Z   Subdivisions, A-Z
Japan
705   General
706.A-Z   Subdivisions, A-Z
Iran
707   General
708.A-Z   Subdivisions, A-Z
Russia in Asia. Siberia
709   General
710.A-Z   Subdivisions, A-Z
Turkey
711   General
712.A-Z   Subdivisions, A-Z
713.A-Z   Other Asian countries, A-Z
Africa
715   General works
Egypt
717   General

Marine engineering
    By region or country
      Africa
        Egypt -- Continued

718.A-Z	Subdivisions, A-Z
719.A-Z	Other African countries, A-Z

      Australia

721	General
722.A-Z	Subdivisions, A-Z
722.5	New Zealand

      Pacific islands

723	General works
724.A-Z	By island or group of islands, A-Z

    Study and teaching
       Including courses for engineers and firemen

725	General works
726	Examinations, questions, etc.

      By region or country

727	United States
728.A-Z	Other regions or countries, A-Z

    Marine machinery industry

729	General works

      By region or country

729.5	United States
729.6.A-Z	Other regions or countries, A-Z

    Marine engines

731	General works
737	Specifications

      United States

737.U4-.U5	Serials
737.U6A-.U6Z	Vessels with name. By name, A-Z

        e.g.

737.U6A6	Anthracite (Steamship)
737.U6P2	Pansy (Lighthouse tender)
737.U7	Vessels without names. By date

        e.g.

737.U7 1883	A dispatch boat
737.U7 1907	Battleship no. 29
738	Model engines
739	Vibration phenomena

        Cf. VM761 Testing of steamships

740	Marine turbines

        Cf. TJ735+ Steam turbines
        Cf. TJ778 Gas turbines
    Marine boilers

741	General works

VM

Marine engineering
Marine engines
Marine boilers -- Continued
743.A-Z   Special types, A-Z
743.B2   Babcock and Wilcox
743.H5   Herreshoff
743.N6   Niclausse
749   Maintenance and care of marine boilers
Including inspection
Cf. TJ289 Manuals for boiler tenders (General)
750   Oil-burning boilers
Including installation, operation, care, repair, etc.
Resistance and propulsion of ships
Cf. VM521+ Means of propulsion
751   General works
Propellers
753   General works
755   Screw propellers
757.A-Z   Other, A-Z
757.C9   Cycloidal propellers
757.S94   Supercavitating propellers
758   Shafts and shafting
759   Gearing
Tests for propulsion, resistance, stability, etc.
Including reports of experimental towing tanks, etc.
761   General works
Trial trips see VM880+
763   General special
Including the operation, care, lubrication, repair, spare
parts, etc., of marine machinery
765   Auxiliary engines
766   Rotors. Rotor ships
767   Donkey engines and other small steam engines
769   Details and accessories peculiar to marine engines and
boilers
770   Gas and oil engines. Gasoline engines. Diesel engines
Engines for launches and motorboats (Gasoline, steam,
etc.)
771   General works
Electric motors see VM347
773   Electric ship propulsion
Cf. VM347 Electric motors
Marine nuclear reactor plants. Marine atomic power plants
774   General works
774.3   Experimental and prototype projects
776   Safety measures

VM

	Marine engineering
	Diving -- Continued
977	History
	Biography
980.A1	Collective
980.A2-Z	Individual, A-Z
981	General works
983	Popular works
984	Juvenile works
	Special types of diving
985	Diving with submarine-armor equipment
	Including description and catalogs of equipment
987	Diving in a diving bell
989	Other (not A-Z)
	Including diving with flexible tubes

	Including history, description, etc.
	Add the appropriate number from this table to the first number of the classification number span to which the table applies
	For technical works, see UB-UH
0	General works
1	General documents
2	Registers. Lists. Rosters
	Infantry
3	General works
3.5	Divisions. By number and author
4	Regiments. By number and author
	Cavalry
5	General works
5.5	Troops. By number and author
	Artillery
6	General works. Field artillery
6.5	Divisions. By letter or number and author
	Coast artillery
7	General works
7.5	Divisions. By letter or number and author
	Anti-aircraft artillery
7.7	General works
7.75	Divisions or groups
8.A-Z	Organizations. By name, A-Z
9	Miscellaneous topics (not A-Z)

TABLES

21	America
	North America
22	General works
	United States
23	General works
23.5	Confederate States
24.A-.W	By state, A-W
25.A-Z	By city, A-Z
	Canada
26	General works
27.A-Z	By state, province, etc., A-Z
27.5	Latin America (General)
	Mexico
28	General works
29.A-Z	By state, province, etc., A-Z
	Central America
30	General works
31.A-Z	By country, A-Z
	West Indies
32	General works
33.A-Z	By country or island, A-Z
	South America
34	General works
	Argentina
36	General works
37.A-Z	By state, province, etc., A-Z
	Bolivia
38	General works
39.A-Z	By state, province, etc., A-Z
	Brazil
41	General works
42.A-Z	By state, province, etc., A-Z
	Chile
43	General works
44.A-Z	By state, province, etc., A-Z
	Colombia
45	General works
46.A-Z	By state, province, etc., A-Z
	Ecuador
47	General works
48.A-Z	By state, province, etc., A-Z
	Guianas
49	General works
49.5	Suriname. Dutch Guiana
50	French Guiana
51	Paraguay
52	Peru

	South America -- Continued
53	Uruguay
54	Venezuela
	Europe
55	General works
57	Great Britain (General)
58	Special periods. By date
59	England and Wales
61	Scotland
63	Northern Ireland
64.A-Z	Cities (or other special), A-Z
	Austria
65	General works
66.A-Z	By state, province, etc., A-Z
	Belgium
67	General works
68.A-Z	By state, province, etc., A-Z
	Denmark
69	General works
70.A-Z	By state, province, etc., A-Z
	France
71	General works
72.A-Z	By state, province, etc., A-Z
	Germany
	Including West Germany
73	General works
74.A-Z	By state, province, etc., A-Z
74.5	East Germany
	Greece
75	General works
76.A-Z	By state, province, etc., A-Z
76.5	Ireland (Eire)
	Netherlands
77	General works
78.A-Z	By state, province, etc., A-Z
	Italy
79	General works
80.A-Z	By state, province, etc., A-Z
	Norway
81	General works
82.A-Z	By state, province, etc., A-Z
	Portugal
83	General works
84.A-Z	By state, province, etc., A-Z
	Soviet Union
85	General works
86.A-Z	By state, province, etc., A-Z

TABLES

	Europe -- Continued
86.5	Scandinavia (General)
	Spain
87	General works
88.A-Z	By state, province, etc., A-Z
	Sweden
89	General works
90.A-Z	By state, province, etc., A-Z
	Switzerland
91	General works
92.A-Z	By state, province, etc., A-Z
	Turkey see U2 111+
95.A-Z	Other European countries, A-Z
	Asia
99	General works
	China
101	General works
102.A-Z	By state, province, etc., A-Z
	India
103	General works
104.A-Z	By state, province, etc., A-Z
	Japan
105	General works
106.A-Z	By state, province, etc., A-Z
	Iran
107	General works
108.A-Z	By state, province, etc., A-Z
	Soviet Union in Asia. Siberia
109	General works
110.A-Z	By state, province, etc., A-Z
	Turkey
111	General works
112.A-Z	By state, province, etc., A-Z
113.A-Z	Other Asian countries, A-Z
	Africa
115	General works
	Egypt
117	General works
118.A-Z	By state, province, etc., A-Z
119.A-Z	Other African countries, A-Z
	Australia
121	General works
122.A-Z	By state, province, etc., A-Z
122.5	New Zealand
	Pacific Islands
123	General works
124.A-Z	By island or group of islands, A-Z

Add the appropriate number from this table to the first number of the
classification number span to which the table applies

0	Supply and transportation departments
1	Pay and allowances
2	Militia
3.A-Z	By province, etc., A-Z

TABLES

.xC1	Regulations. By date
.xH1	Registers. By date
.xL1	History. By date
.xR1	Miscellaneous topics. By date

.xA1-.xA19	Periodicals. Serials
.xC1	Regulations. By date
.xH1	Registers. By date
.xL1	History. By date
.xR1	Miscellaneous topics. By date

TABLES

Boats, Fishing: VM431
Boats, Folding: VM357
Boats, Hydrofoil: VM362
Boats, Inflatable: VM360
Boats, Jet: VM348.5
Boats, Lifesaving: VK1473
Boats, Pilot: VM466.P54
Boats, Scout (War vessels): V880+
Boats, Submarine: V857+
  Construction: VM365+
Boats, Toy: VM359
Boatswains: VG950+
Boatswains' mates: VG950+
Boatyards: VM321.5+
Boilers, Marine: VM741+
Boilers, Oil-burning (Ships): VM750
Bombers: UG1242.B6
Bombing
  Air warfare: UG700+
Bombs
  Air forces: UG1280+
  Aircraft projectiles: UF767
Bombsights: UG1272.B65
Booms (Ship-loading apparatus):
  VM831
Border patrols: UA12.83
Border troops: UA12.83
Bottlenose dolphins
  Military service: UH100.5.B67
Bounties, Military: UB370+
Bounties, Naval: VB280+
Bows
  Military science: U877+
Boy scouts (Sea scouting): VK544
Boys
  Military administration: UB418.C45
Boys' units
  Military education
    Great Britain: U549.2+
Bremen (Passenger ship): VM383.B7
Brevets
  Air forces: UG976+
  Marines: VE495+
  Military administration: UB430+
  Naval administration: VB330+
Bridge lights (Navigation): VK1247+

Bridge troops
  Military engineering: UG510+
Bridges
  Military engineering: UG335
Broadsword exercises
  Military science: U870
Browning machine guns: UF620.B6
Budgets, Cost of: UA17
Bugeyes: VM311.B8
Building appliances
  Marine engineering: VM901+
Building, Military: UG460
Buildings
  Military: UH470+
Bulk carriers (Cargo ships): VM393.B7
Bulkhead construction (Ships): VM469
Bulletproof clothing: UF910
Bulletproof materials: UF910
Bullets
  Naval ordnance: VF500
  Ordnance: UF770
Bunkering facilities
  Docks: VK361+
Bunkers
  Military engineering: UG405.15
Buoyance of ships: VM157
Buoys and buoyage
  Lifesaving apparatus: VK1475
  Lighthouse service: VK1000+
Bureaus, Hydrographic: VK596
Buttons
  Military maintenance: UC487,
    UC487.5

C

Cable ships: VM466.C3
Cables
  Marine engineering: VM791
  Naval maintenance: VC279.C3
Caïques
  Construction: VM311.C24
Caissons
  Artillery: UF640+
California (Battleship): VA65.C3
Camel batteries: UF420
Camel troops: UE500

Wooden ships: VM142+
Wounded, Care of
  Military: UH520+

Y

Yachts: VM331+
Yeomen: VG900+
Yukon (Steamer): VM461.5.Y84

GPO U.S. GOVERNMENT PRINTING OFFICE: 2008–340–014/60024